Text by
Beverley Piper

Photography by
Peter Barry

Designed by
Philip Clucas

Produced by
Ted Smart and Gerald Hughes

Editorial Direction
David Gibbon

MICROWAVE
COOKING

Exeter Books

NEW YORK

Contents

Introduction

The microwave oven is one of the most exciting kitchen appliances available. It may be used to defrost, reheat, and cook foods, and is therefore more versatile than a conventional oven; in fact it can cope with 75% of your normal cooking needs.

The theory behind microwave cooking must be learned and fully understood before a microwave oven can be used to its full extent. It is a very different method of cooking, which is clean, quick, efficient, labor saving and economical.

The Principles of Microwave Cookery

Electricity is converted into microwave energy inside the oven by the magnetron. The 'microwaves' are transferred into the oven cavity where they bounce off the metal interior and penetrate the outer 1"-1½" of the food. They pass through non-metal containers as though they were not there, and simply cause the molecules in the food to vibrate very fast indeed. The heat that is created passes by conduction through to the center of the food and the food is cooked by friction heat. As a rough guide, cooking times by the microwave method are about ⅓ to ¼ of the conventional times.

Different Types of Microwave Ovens

A microwave oven may be either free standing or built-in. If built-in, it is placed in a housing unit, with a conventional oven situated above or below the microwave.

Convected Hot Air and Microwave Combined

These ovens are now widely available. They are more expensive than an ordinary microwave oven as they combine two units in one. The most common criticism of food cooked in a microwave is that it does not appear 'brown'. This is because there is no dry heat available to caramelise or 'brown' the food. Some people prefer to buy the combination ovens, which use traditional cooking methods and microwave cooking combined. In some models both cooking methods may be used simultaneously, whilst in others the

microwave and the hot air ovens are used one after the other.

Broilers
Some microwave ovens offer a browning broiler.

The Output of the Microwave
The cooking time for each dish/recipe is governed by the electrical output of the microwave oven, and the output also controls the running costs of the appliance. The output is measured in watts. A 700w microwave oven consumes about 1.3k per hour and is, therefore, a most economical method of cooking. Microwave ovens are available in a variety of power ratings and the cooking, re-heating and defrosting times vary according to the output. A 3lb chicken takes 21 minutes in a 700w microwave and 28 minutes in a 500w.

There is no pre-heating before use, and no cooling down after cooking.

Versatility
A microwave oven may be used to defrost, cook and reheat food. It is also well suited to the many different methods of cooking – a microwave oven can poach, shallow fat fry, braise, roast, boil and bake. It will even dry herbs for winter use, and may be used to sterilize jars. The oven and cooking containers stay cool, and microwave ovens are, therefore, perfectly safe for elderly people to use, and for households where there are children.

Cleaning
As the oven cabinet does not get very hot, all that is necessary is a

wipe with a clean dish cloth. Should smells cling e.g. curry or fish, simply squeeze a lemon into 1¾ cups of water and bring to the boil. Wipe the oven with the acidulated water. Food does not bake onto the containers so they are easier to wash up.

Turntables

Manufacturers choose different methods of ensuring that the food cooks evenly. Go by personal recommendation wherever possible. Hidden turntables are popular as they do not restrict the shape of dish used. Some ovens offer stirrer fans and turntables.

Standing Times

Standing, or equalizing, time is simply the time that the food takes to finish cooking. The heat is passed from the outside to the center by conduction. The standing time will vary according to the size and density of the food. Standing time may take place either inside or outside the microwave oven; it is an important part of microwave cookery which must be used. It is just as important after defrosting.

Containers for Use in the Microwave Oven

Special containers are available for microwave cookery, but they are

not essential. The heat is localized in the food, and not in the container, so the dish itself does not usually become hot. Some plastics, Pyrex, china, glass, and even paper and basketware, may be used. Be guided by the length of time the food will stand in the microwave, and by the temperature that it will reach.

Plastic wrap is a boon to the microwave owner, as it may be used in place of a lid to cover foods and prevent splashing. Do remember to pierce plastic wrap and roasta bags to allow steam to escape.

Metal – including tin foil – may damage the heart of the microwave oven, the magnetron, and should not be used unless specifically directed by the manufacturer.

Browning Dish or Skillet

A browning dish is a special dish which, when preheated in the microwave oven, will become very hot over the base. Several shapes and sizes are available, either with a lid or without. The dish is used to brown such foods as chops, sausages, hamburgers, bacon, eggs etc. The food must be turned to brown on the other side. The deep browning dishes with lids are also used as casserole dishes. *These containers must not be used in conventional ovens.*

**Herby Roast Chicken (left),
Devilled Pork Chops (below)
and Chicken Breasts in Garlic
Cream Sauce (right).**

Variable Power Chart

MICROWAVE POWER LEVEL	DESCRIPTION AND SUGGESTED USE
10 or Full–High	Microwave energy constant at full wattage. For cooking vegetables, poultry, fish and some sauces, start joints.
8 or Roast	Power on for 13 seconds, auto cut-out for 2 seconds. Repeated continually for time selected, for reheating some joints.
7 and 6 – Medium	Power is on for about 10 seconds, off for 5 seconds, for chops, meat balls, chicken pieces, cakes.
4 and 5 – Simmer	Power is on for 6 seconds, off for 9 seconds, for completing casseroles, defrosting large joints, egg and cheese dishes.
3 – Defrost	Generally for defrosting (allow a standing time afterwards), for melting chocolate, and for delicate sauces.
2 – Very Low	Power is on for 3 seconds, off for 12 seconds. Keep cooked food warm for up to ½ hour. Soften butter and cream cheese from refrigerator.

Please note that this chart is given only as a guide. The variable power dial differs slightly from manufacturer to manufacturer.

Cooked food reheats remarkably quickly without drying out. A chart is provided to give some of the most common foods. Allow a few minutes standing time, after reheating, and before serving.

GENERAL RULES FOR REHEATING.
1. <u>Cover food</u>, allowing steam to escape, unless told specifically not to cover.
2. <u>Stir</u> foods such as casseroles, baked beans, stewed fruits, halfway through reheating.
3. Allow a short <u>standing time</u> – 3- 5 minutes before removing covering and serving.
4. Reheat small items, such as sausage rolls or sausages, arranged in <u>ring fashion</u> on outside edge of plate. Reheat on Power 4, or Simmer.

Re-heating Chart

TYPE OF FOOD & WEIGHT	COVER	STIRRING	POWER LEVEL	TIME
1 Plated Meal	Plastic Wrap	–	Full	3-4 minutes
1 Large Macaroni Cheese	Plastic Wrap	Yes, once	Power 7 or Roast	10 minutes
2 Bowls Soup	–	Yes, once	Full	5 minutes
Baked Beans 4ozs	–	–	Power 7 or Roast	2 minutes
Baked Beans 16ozs	Yes	Yes, twice	Power 7 or Roast	7 minutes
Chicken Pieces 8ozs	Yes	–	Full	3-4 minutes
Beef Casserole For 4	Yes	Yes, twice	Full	10-12 minutes
Cooked Vegetables 4ozs	Yes	–	Full	45 seconds
Cooked Vegetables 1lb	Yes	Yes, once	Full	2 minutes
1 Family Meat Pie	No	No	4 or Simmer	7-8 minutes
6 Mince Pies	No	No	4 or Simmer	4 minutes
4 Bread Rolls	Kitchen Roll	No	4 or Simmer	2 minutes
Christmas Pudding 1½lb	Plastic Wrap	No	Power 7 or Roast	3 minutes
Sauce ½ pt	Plastic Wrap	Yes, twice	Full	2 minutes
Fish 12ozs	Plastic Wrap	–	Full	2 minutes

Defrosting Chart

FOOD TO BE DEFROSTED AND WEIGHT	POWER LEVEL	MICROWAVE TIME	STANDING TIME
Ground Meat 1lb	4 or defrost	6 minutes	15 minutes
Chicken 3lb	4 or defrost	30 minutes	30 minutes
Joint of Beef 3lb	4 or defrost	20 minutes	30 minutes
Shepherd's Pie 1lb	4 or defrost	8 minutes	10 minutes
Large Lasagne	6 or simmer	20 minutes	15 minutes
Chops 1lb	4 or defrost	6 minutes	10 minutes
Sausages 1lb	4 or defrost	6 minutes	10 minutes
Cod 8ozs	4 or defrost	6 minutes	10 minutes
Raspberries 8ozs	4 or defrost	4 minutes	15 minutes
1 Victoria Sandwich (2 egg)	4 or defrost	2-3 minutes	15 minutes
Large Sliced Loaf	4 or defrost	7 minutes	10 minutes
Cheese Sauce ½ Pint	4 or defrost	7 minutes	7 minutes
Chicken in Sauce for 4	Simmer	12 minutes	10 minutes
Family Apple Pie	4 or defrost	8 minutes	5 minutes
Family Meat Pie or Quiche Lorraine	4 or defrost	6-7 minutes	10 minutes

The microwave oven makes a perfect partner for your freezer as it enables you to defrost frozen foods in a fraction of the time that it would normally take. Remember to turn or stir the foods, for more even defrosting, and remember that a standing time is very important.

ALTERING TIMINGS

The recipes given in this book can be cooked in any model of variable power microwave oven that is available today. Each of these recipes was tested in a 700W microwave oven. Convert the timings in the following way, if the output of your oven is other than 700W:–

If using an oven of 500W, add 40 seconds for each minute stated in the recipe.

If using an oven of 600W, add 20 seconds for each minute stated in the recipe.

If using an oven of 650W plus, you will only need to allow a slight increase in the overall time.

Stirring and Turning

Stirring and turning are methods used to equalize the heat in the food, i.e. the cooking of the food. The amount of stirring or turning will be governed by the type of food to be cooked, the cooking time and the even distribution of energy in the microwave oven. The recipes in this book give you a guide as to when to stir and turn. Adjust, if necessary, according to your own particular oven. Arrange foods such as baked apples or jacket potatoes in a ring fashion, leaving a space in the center.

Starting Temperature of Food

The starting temperature of food will alter the cooking time. It may be at average room temperature, at cold room temperature or taken from the refrigerator or cold larder. Please note that the timings in this book are calculated for food at average room temperature, unless otherwise stated.

Can You Cook a Complete Meal by Microwave?

The easiest way to use a microwave oven is to employ stage cookery.

The microwave oven cooks according to weight and time, not by temperature, and different types of food require different cooking times. During the standing time of the denser foods, such as joints and jacket potatoes, the less dense items, such as vegetables and sauces, are completely cooked. Foods of similar density may be cooked together, e.g. potatoes and carrots, but remember that the total energy available in the microwave oven must be shared between the foods introduced. If carrots and potatoes are cooked simultaneously, the resulting weight must be checked, and the cooking time calculated accordingly.

Some Things Cannot be Done

Do not try to cook Yorkshire puddings or other batter recipes, boil eggs, deep fat fry, or produce really crisp foods such as roast potatoes, as none of these will be successful. *Pastry* – baking blind, suet crust and some puff pastry recipes work beautifully, but do not try to cook the top of an apple pie.

Soups and Starters

Vegetable Soup

PREPARATION TIME: 10 minutes
MICROWAVE TIME: 21-26 minutes
SERVES: 4 people

2 tblsp butter
1lb young leeks, cleaned and sliced
1 medium onion, peeled and sliced
1½ cups potato, peeled and diced
1 carrot, peeled and diced
Salt and freshly ground black pepper
  to taste
1¼ tblsp chopped fresh parsley
1¾ cups homemade chicken stock
1¼ cups milk

Melt the butter in a 3 quart casserole dish. Microwave on Full Power for 1 minute. Stir in all the prepared vegetables, salt and pepper, parsley and 4 tblsp of the stock. Cover the dish, piercing the plastic wrap if used. Microwave on Full Power for 12 minutes. Stir. Set aside, covered, for 5 minutes. Transfer the vegetables into the food processor bowl or blender goblet; add the milk and blend or process until smooth. Return to the casserole dish and stir in the remaining stock. Microwave on Full Power, covered, for 3-5 minutes. Stir well before serving.

Asparagus with Mayonnaise

PREPARATION TIME: 10 minutes
MICROWAVE TIME: 10-12 minutes
SERVES: 4 people

1lb frozen asparagus spears
1 cup corn oil
2 tblsp butter
1 egg
1 egg yolk
⅔ cup olive oil
Salt and freshly ground black pepper
  to taste
2½ tblsp lemon juice
Chopped fresh parsley

Arrange the asparagus in a roasta bag in a suitable dish. Add 4 tblsp water to the bag, with the butter. Seal the bag with a rubber band.

Pierce the bag once at the base. Microwave on Full Power for 10-12 minutes, turning the bag over once halfway through cooking time. Set aside. Put the egg and egg yolk into the goblet of a food processor or blender with the salt and pepper. Blend on maximum. Add the oil, in a steady trickle, blending to a smooth mayonnaise. Add the lemon juice. Carefully drain the asparagus and arrange on a heated serving dish. Sprinkle with the parsley and serve accompanied by the mayonnaise. Serve immediately.

Soured Cream Prawns

PREPARATION TIME: 5 minutes
MICROWAVE TIME: 7-8 minutes
SERVES: 4 people

4 tblsp butter
2 cups peeled shrimps
Freshly ground black pepper to taste
1 egg yolk
⅔ cup soured cream
Paprika

Butter 4 ramekin dishes and divide the shrimps among them. Season well with black pepper. Combine the egg yolk and soured cream and spoon over the shrimps. Dot with the remaining butter. Microwave all 4 ramekins together on Power 4, or Simmer, for 7-8 minutes. (The dishes should be arranged in a ring, leaving a space in the centre.) Serve immediately sprinkled with paprika.

Corn Starter

PREPARATION TIME: 5 minutes
MICROWAVE TIME: 15 minutes
SERVES: 4 people

4 corn cobs
Sprigs of fresh savory
Salt and freshly ground black pepper
  to taste
A stick of butter

Arrange the cobs in a suitable dish. Add 3 tblsp cold water and a few sprigs of savory. Season. Cover with plastic wrap and pierce.

Microwave on Full Power for 6 minutes. Turn each cob over. Recover and microwave on Full Power for 6 minutes. Set aside. Put the butter into a 1¼ pint jug and microwave on Power 4 or Simmer for about 3 minutes or until melted. Transfer the cooked cobs to a serving dish. Pour over the butter and sprinkle with extra chopped savory before serving.

Individual Frozen Pizzas

PREPARATION TIME: 2 minutes
MICROWAVE TIME: 6½-8½ minutes
SERVES: 1 person

Preheat a browning dish, without the lid, for 5-7 minutes. Put 1¼ tblsp of oil and 1 individual pizza onto the dish. Microwave uncovered for approximately 1½ minutes on Full Power. Allow to stand for 1 minute before serving. As many pizzas as will fit onto your dish may be microwaved at the same time; increase the microwave time accordingly. Pizzas may be heated directly from the freezer, without the browning dish, on an ordinary non-metallic plate but the base will not be as crisp.

Chestnut Soup

PREPARATION TIME: 15 minutes
MICROWAVE TIME: 34 minutes
SERVES: 4 people

2 tblsp butter
1 stalk celery, chopped
2 large onions, chopped
3¾ cups homemade chicken stock
  (hot)
8oz unsweetened chestnut puree
Salt and freshly ground black pepper
  to taste
4 rashers bacon, de-rinded

Put the butter, celery and onions into a 3 quart casserole dish; cover with a lid and microwave on Full Power for 4 minutes. Stir. Mix 1¼ cups stock with the chestnut puree, in a 2½ pint mixing bowl. Stir into the onion mixture. Season

with salt and black pepper; cover and microwave on Full Power for 7 minutes. Stir in the remaining stock and microwave on Full Power for 20 minutes. Allow to stand whilst preparing the bacon. Arrange the bacon on a microwave roasting rack, or on 2 sheets of absorbent kitchen paper. Microwave, uncovered, on Full Power, for about 3 minutes. Serve the soup sprinkled with the crumbled crispy bacon.

Tomato Baskets

PREPARATION TIME: 5 minutes
MICROWAVE TIME: 5½-6½ minutes
SERVES: 6 people

6 large firm tomatoes
8oz packet frozen mixed vegetables
4 tblsp butter
Salt and freshly ground black pepper
  to taste
Few sprigs of fresh mint

Cut the top off each tomato and reserve. Using a grapefruit knife or a teaspoon, carefully scoop out the centre flesh. (Use in a soup or sauce recipe). Pierce the pouch of frozen vegetables once and place in a dish. Microwave on Full Power for 3½ minutes, turning the bag once halfway through the cooking time. Set aside. Stand the prepared tomatoes upright on a serving dish, in a ring. Dot with half the butter.

Asparagus with Mayonnaise (top), Vegetable Soup (center) and Soured Cream Prawns (bottom).

Microwave on Full Power for about 2-3 minutes until very hot. Mix the drained, cooked vegetables with the remaining butter and salt and pepper and spoon into the tomato shells. Top with the reserved lids, and garnish with sprigs of mint. Serve immediately.

Quick Flat Bun Pizzas

PREPARATION TIME: 10 minutes
MICROWAVE TIME: 6½-7½ minutes
SERVES: 4 as a main meal, 8 as a snack

4 flat buns
1 medium onion, finely chopped
1¼ tsp tomato paste
1¼ tsp dried oregano
8oz can tomatoes, chopped
1¼ tsp French mustard
Salt and freshly ground black pepper to taste
1¼ cups Cheddar cheese, thinly sliced or grated
Stuffed olives, sliced

Tomato Baskets (right), Quick Flat Bun Pizzas (below) and Individual Frozen Pizza (far right).

Cut the flat buns in half and arrange in a ring on a suitable cooky sheet. Place the onion in a 2½ pint mixing bowl; cover and microwave for 1½ minutes on Full Power. Stir in the tomato paste, oregano, chopped tomatoes and the mustard. Season with salt and pepper. Divide among the flat buns, and cover with the cheese. Decorate with the sliced olives. Microwave on Power 4 for 5-6 minutes, until the cheese has melted. Serve immediately.

Garlic Prawn Starter

PREPARATION TIME: 30 minutes
MICROWAVE TIME: 20 minutes
SERVES: 4 people

1½lb zucchini, cleaned, topped and tailed
Salt and freshly ground black pepper to taste
12oz peeled prawns
1¼ tblsp chopped chives
2½ tblsp dry white wine
2 cloves garlic, crushed
1¼ tblsp lemon juice
4 tblsp butter

Garnish
Unpeeled prawns

Slice the zucchini thinly into a colander, sprinkling them generously with salt. Cover with a plate and weigh down; leave to stand for 20 minutes. Rinse well under cold running water. Drain thoroughly. Arrange the zucchini in a vegetable dish. Season with salt and pepper. Cover and microwave on Full Power for 12 minutes. Stir. Set aside, covered. Put the peeled prawns, chives, wine, garlic, lemon juice and butter into a 2½ pint casserole dish . Cover with a lid. Microwave on Power 4, or Simmer, for 8 minutes. Stir once halfway through cooking time. Drain the excess liquid from the zucchini. Top with the heated prawns and their juices. Garnish with the unpeeled prawns and serve immediately.

Egg and Tuna Starter

PREPARATION TIME: 10 minutes

MICROWAVE TIME: 10 minutes

SERVES: 4 people

7oz can tuna fish in oil, drained
2 hard boiled eggs, cooked
   conventionally and chopped
1 cup milk
2 tblsp butter
Salt and freshly ground black pepper
   to taste
¼ cup all purpose flour
1¼ tsp made mustard
½ cup grated Cheddar cheese

Garnish
Stuffed olives, sliced

Flake the tuna fish and divide between 4 ramekin dishes. Top with the egg. Melt the butter in a 1 litre jug for 1 minute on Full Power, or until very hot. Stir in the flour and gradually stir in the milk. Microwave on Full Power for 2 minutes. Beat well with a wire whisk. Microwave on Full Power for 2 minutes. Beat well with a wire whisk. Beat in salt and pepper and cheese. Divide the sauce among the ramekins. Garnish with sliced olives. Microwave all 4 ramekins together for 5 minutes on Power 4 or Simmer. Serve immediately.

Mackerel Pate

PREPARATION TIME: 10 minutes,
                              plus chilling

MICROWAVE TIME: 3 minutes

SERVES: 6 people

1 onion, finely chopped
4 tblsp butter
1½ cups cream cheese
2½ tblsp lemon juice
2½ tblsp chopped fresh parsley

¾lb smoked mackerel fillets
1¼ tsp coarse French mustard
Freshly ground black pepper to taste
4 tblsp soured cream
2½ tsp tomato paste

Garnish
Lemon wedges
Fresh parsley and cucumber slices

Put the onion into a soup bowl. Cover with plastic wrap and pierce. Microwave on Full Power for 1 minute. Set aside. Flake the fish into the food processor or blender goblet, discarding skin and bones. Add the onion. Place the butter in the bowl used for the onion and microwave on Power 4, or Simmer, for 2 minutes. Add to the processor or blender with all the remaining ingredients. Process or blend until smooth. Pour into a dampened loaf pan; smooth the surface. Chill until firm. Turn out onto a serving dish and garnish with wedges of lemon, crimped cucumber slices and parsley.

This page: Corn Starter (top), Garlic Prawn Starter (bottom).

Facing Page: Chestnut Soup (top left), Egg and Tuna Starter (top right) and Mackerel Pate (bottom).

Vegetables

All types of vegetables, both frozen and fresh, microwave exceptionally well. They keep their color, flavor and shape. Follow a few simple rules and use the charts to help you.

Helpful Hints
1. If you want to add salt, dissolve it in a little water beforehand. Adding salt can cause some vegetables to dry; to be on the safe side season with salt after cooking.
2. Always cover vegetables – roasta or freezer bags are very useful, but remember to pierce them.
3. Stir at least once during the cooking time or, if using a bag, turn it over.
4. Add only the amount of water necessary.
5. Cut the vegetables into even sized pieces.
6. Allow a standing time after cooking and before serving.
7. Cook frozen vegetables from frozen, do not defrost them first.

Fresh Vegetable Chart

VEGETABLE AND WEIGHT	ADDITION	MICROWAVE TIME	STANDING TIME
Sliced Green Beans 1lb	4 tblsp water	8 minutes	5 minutes
Broad Beans 1lb	4 tblsp water	8 minutes	5 minutes
Broccoli Spears 8ozs	4 tblsp water	7 minutes	4 minutes
Sliced Carrots 1lb	2½ tblsp water	7-8 minutes	4 minutes
Cauliflower Flowerets 1lb	4 tblsp water	7-8 minutes	5 minutes
Chopped Celery 8ozs		7 minutes	4 minutes
Zucchini 1lb	2 tblsp butter	10 minutes	3 minutes
Leeks 1lb	2½ tblsp water	7-8 minutes	3 minutes
Mushrooms (Sliced) 8ozs	2 tblsp butter	2 minutes	2 minutes
Sliced Summer Squash 1lb	2 tblsp butter	7 minutes	3 minutes
New Potatoes 1lb	2½ tblsp water	7 minutes	4 minutes
Old Potatoes 1lb	4 tblsp water	9 minutes	5 minutes
Sliced Onions 1lb	2½ tblsp water	8-9 minutes	4 minutes
Brussels Sprouts 1lb	2½ tblsp water	6-7 minutes	4 minutes
Diced Swede 1lb	2½ tblsp water	13 minutes	6 minutes

Baked Stuffed Summer Squash

PREPARATION TIME: 20 minutes
MICROWAVE TIME: 22 minutes
SERVES: 4 people

1 medium size summer squash
2 tblsp butter
1 onion, peeled and finely chopped
1lb raw, lean ground beef
2 tblsp all purpose flour
1½ tsp dried basil or oregano
1 egg, beaten
1 beef stock cube, crumbled
Salt and freshly ground black pepper to taste
1¼ tblsp tomato paste

Wipe the summer squash with a damp cloth. Cut both ends off the summer squash and keep on one side. Scoop out the seeds with a spoon and discard. Melt the butter in a 2 quart mixing bowl for 1 minute on Full Power. Stir in the onion. Microwave on Full Power for 1 minute. Stir in all the remaining ingredients. Mix well. Secure one end of the summer squash with wooden cocktail

sticks. Stuff the summer squash with the mixture. Secure the remaining end in place with wooden cocktail sticks. Place the summer squash on a meat roasting rack and cover with plastic wrap. Pierce. Microwave on Full Power for about 20 minutes, turning the summer squash once halfway through cooking time. Allow to stand, covered with foil, for 5 minutes before serving. Cut into rings, and serve piping hot.

Brussels Sprouts with Chestnut and Bacon

PREPARATION TIME: 15 minutes
MICROWAVE TIME: 8 minutes
SERVES: 4 people

1lb fresh Brussels sprouts
1¼ tblsp lemon juice
1½ tsp dried mixed herbs
2½ tblsp cold water
Salt and freshly ground black pepper to taste
6 tblsp butter
8oz canned whole chestnuts, drained
3 rashers bacon, de-rinded, cooked and chopped (see Garlic Mushrooms recipe)

Peel the sprouts and make a cross in the base of each one. Put the sprouts into a 2½ pint casserole dish, or into a roasta bag. Add the lemon juice, herbs, water, and salt and pepper. Cover with a lid, or pierce the bag if used. Microwave on Full Power for 5 minutes. Stir or turn once, halfway through cooking time. Set aside for 5 minutes. Put the butter into a ¾

pint jug and microwave on Power 4 or Simmer until melted (about 3 minutes). If using a roasta bag, tip the sprouts into serving dish. Add the chestnuts to the Brussels sprouts, stirring gently. Cover with a lid. Microwave on Full Power for 1 minute. Coat with melted butter, sprinkle with chopped bacon, and serve.

Brussels Sprouts with Chestnut and Bacon (top), Carrot and Parsnip Puree (center) and Baked Stuffed Summer Squash (bottom).

Frozen Vegetable Chart

VEGETABLE AND WEIGHT	AMOUNT OF WATER	COOKING TIME	STANDING TIME
Asparagus 8ozs	2½ tblsp	7 minutes	5 minutes
Broccoli 8ozs	4 tblsp	10 minutes	5 minutes
Brussels Sprouts 8ozs	2½ tblsp	4 minutes	3 minutes
Carrots 8ozs	2½ tblsp	6 minutes	3 minutes
Cauli Flowerets 8ozs	2½ tblsp	3 minutes	2 minutes
Zucchini 8ozs	Nil	4 minutes	2 minutes
Leeks 8ozs	2½ tblsp	6-7 minutes	2 minutes
Mixed Vegetables 8ozs	2½ tblsp	4 minutes	3 minutes
Mushrooms 8ozs	2 tblsp butter and herbs	4 minutes	2 minutes
Baby Onions 8ozs	2 tblsp butter	5 minutes	4 minutes
Peas 8ozs	Nil	4 minutes	2 minutes
Spinach 8ozs	Nil	5 minutes	3 minutes
Corn 8ozs	Nil	4 minutes	2 minutes

Carrot and Parsnip Puree

PREPARATION TIME: 15 minutes

MICROWAVE TIME: 13 minutes

SERVES: 4 people

8oz carrots, peeled
8oz parsnips, peeled
1 level tsp dried basil
4 tblsp well-flavored stock
2½ tblsp heavy cream
Salt and freshly ground black pepper
  to taste
Pinch grated nutmeg

Garnish
Carrot curls

Dice the peeled carrots and parsnips and place in a roasta bag in a 2½ pint casserole dish. Add 2½ tblsp water and the basil. Snip the bag once at the base. Microwave on Full Power for 8 minutes, turning the bag over once halfway through cooking time. Set aside for 5 minutes. Empty the contents of the roasta bag into the goblet of a food processor or blender. Add the stock and process until smooth. Add cream, salt and pepper, and nutmeg. Process just to

blend. Return to the casserole dish and cover with a lid. Microwave on Power 4, or Simmer, for 5 minutes. Garnish with carrot curls and serve.

Zucchini Choice

PREPARATION TIME: 40-45 minutes

COOKING TIME: 10 minutes

SERVES: 4 people

1lb young zucchini, topped, tailed
  and washed
Salt and freshly ground black pepper
  to taste
1lb large firm tomatoes, skinned and
  sliced
1 tsp dried tarragon
1 clove garlic, crushed
2 tblsp butter

Arrange the sliced zucchini in a colander. Sprinkle generously with salt and leave to stand for 30 minutes. (This draws out the bitter juices.) Rinse well under cold running water. Drain. Layer the zucchini and tomatoes in a 2½ pint casserole dish, starting and finishing with zucchini. Season

each layer with salt, pepper, tarragon and garlic. Dot the top with small knobs of butter. Cover tightly with a lid. Microwave on Full Power for 10 minutes. Allow to stand for 3 minutes before serving.

Cauliflower Cheese

PREPARATION TIME: 10 minutes

MICROWAVE TIME: 12 minutes

SERVES: 4 people

1 cauliflower, trimmed and divided
  into flowerets
1½ tblsp cornstarch
1¼ cups milk
1¼ tsp made mustard
Salt and freshly ground black pepper
  to taste
¾ cup grated Cheddar cheese
2 tblsp butter
½ red pepper, de-seeded and chopped

Arrange the flowerets of cauliflower in a roasta bag. Add 3 tblsp water. Pierce the bag, and place in a 2½ pint casserole dish. Microwave on Full Power for 7-8 minutes, turning the bag over once

halfway through cooking time. Set aside, covered. Cream the cornstarch with a little of the milk to a smooth paste. Stir in the mustard and salt and pepper to taste. Heat the remaining milk in a 2¼ pint jug for 2 minutes on Full Power. Pour the heated milk onto the cornstarch mixture, stirring continuously. Return to the jug and microwave on Full Power for 2 minutes or until boiling. Beat in the cheese and butter, and any liquid from the cauliflower. Transfer cauliflower flowerets to a warmed serving dish. Pour the sauce over evenly. Sprinkle with the red pepper and serve immediately. The red pepper may be heated in a cup in the microwave for 1 minute on Full Power, if liked.

Ratatouille

PREPARATION TIME: 40 minutes

MICROWAVE TIME: 22-24 minutes

SERVES: 4 people

½lb zucchini
1lb eggplant
Salt and freshly ground black pepper
  to taste
4 tblsp butter
1 medium onion, peeled and sliced
1 large clove garlic, crushed
A little oil
1 red pepper, de-seeded and sliced
15oz can tomatoes, chopped
½ tsp dried oregano
½ cup crumbled Danish Blue cheese

Wash the zucchini and eggplant. Cut off the ends and discard. Slice into ¼ inch slices and layer with a generous sprinkling of salt in a colander. Top with a plate and a weight and set aside to drain for 15 minutes. Rinse well under cold running water and drain. Put the butter in a 1¼ pint measuring jug. Microwave on Full Power for 1-2 minutes until melted. Stir in the onion and garlic. Grease the sides and base of a 2-3 quart casserole or souffle dish with oil. Layer the eggplant, zucchini and red pepper

Ratatouille (top), Zucchini Choice (center left) and Cauliflower Cheese (bottom).

in the dish with the tomatoes, oregano, onion and garlic. Season each layer with salt and pepper. Cover with a lid. Microwave on Full Power for 20-22 minutes, removing the lid for the last 8 minutes. Turn the dish ¼ turn twice during the cooking time, if necessary. Top with the crumbled cheese and serve immediately.

Buttery Mashed Potato

PREPARATION TIME: 10 minutes
MICROWAVE TIME: 17 minutes
SERVES: 4-5 people

2lb old potatoes, peeled
4 tblsp milk
4 tblsp butter
Salt and freshly ground black pepper
* to taste*
2½ tblsp light cream
Chopped fresh parsley

Cut the potatoes into small, even sized pieces and put into a roasta bag with the milk and butter. Season. Secure the bag with an elastic band and stand in a 2 quart mixing bowl. Pierce the bag once at the base. Microwave on Full Power for 17 minutes, turning the bag over once halfway through the cooking time. Allow to stand for 5 minutes. Turn the potatoes and their liquid into the bowl and mash with a fork. Beat with a wooden spoon adding the cream. Turn into a serving dish. Fork up and sprinkle with the parsley. Serve.

Potatoes Gratinee

PREPARATION TIME: 20 minutes
MICROWAVE TIME: 26 minutes
SERVES: 4 people

1½lb old white potatoes, peeled and
* thinly sliced*
1¼ cups pouring white sauce
½ cup grated cheese
4 tblsp milk
Salt and freshly ground black pepper
* to taste*
2 tblsp butter
1 Recipe quantity of Crispy Topping
* (see recipe)*

Soak the potato slices in cold water for a few minutes. Heat the sauce in a large jug for 1 minute on Full Power. Beat in the grated cheese, milk, and salt and pepper to taste. Grease a shallow dish with the butter. Arrange the drained potato slices, overlapping slightly, in the

Spinach Fiesta (top), Buttery Mashed Potato (far left) and Potatoes Gratinee (left).

base of the dish. Pour the sauce evenly over the top. Cover with plastic wrap and pierce. Microwave on Power 7, or Roast, for 25 minutes. Stir once, gently, halfway through cooking time. Serve after 5 minutes standing time, sprinkled with the crispy topping.

Stuffed Baked Peppers

PREPARATION TIME: 10 minutes

MICROWAVE TIME: 14½-15½ minutes

SERVES: 4 people

4 large even-sized peppers, about 8oz each
3 tblsp water
¾lb cooked chicken, pork or turkey
3 tblsp drained, canned corn kernels
5 tblsp soured cream
¾ cup chopped mushrooms
Salt and freshly ground black pepper to taste

Cut the tops off the peppers and reserve. Scoop out the seeds and discard them. Stand the peppers upright in an oblong or round casserole dish. Add the water; cover and microwave on Full Power for 3½ minutes. Set aside. Combine all the remaining ingredients to make the filling and mix well. Drain the water from the peppers and divide the filling among them. Replace the tops. Cover with plastic wrap and pierce. Microwave on Full Power for 11-12 minutes. Stand for 3 minutes before serving.

Garlic Mushrooms

PREPARATION TIME: 20 minutes

MICROWAVE TIME: 12½-14½ minutes

SERVES: 4 people

6 tblsp butter
2 cloves garlic, crushed
¾lb mushrooms, stalks removed
4 rashers bacon, de-rinded
1 cup cream cheese
Salt and freshly ground black pepper to taste
1½ tblsp natural yogurt or soured cream
¾ tsp dried parsley

Garnish
Chopped fresh parsley

Place the butter and garlic into a small bowl and microwave on Power 4, or Simmer, for 3 minutes, or until melted. Using a pastry brush, brush the mushrooms all over, inside and out, with the melted butter. Arrange on a dinner plate, or cooky sheet, in a circular fashion, leaving a space in the centre. Arrange the bacon on 2 sheets of absorbent kitchen paper, on a dinner plate, fat to outside. Cover with 1 piece absorbent kitchen paper. Microwave the bacon on Full Power for 2½-3 minutes. Set aside. Transfer the cream cheese to a 2½ pint mixing bowl. Microwave, uncovered, on Defrost for 2 minutes. Stir in salt and pepper to taste, yogurt, dried parsley and chopped bacon. Soften the chopped onion in a cup for 45 seconds on Full Power. Stir into the cream cheese mixture. Fill the mushrooms with the cheese mixture. Microwave, uncovered on Roast, or Power 7, for 4-6 minutes. Serve immediately garnished with chopped parsley, on croutons of fried bread.

Spinach Fiesta

PREPARATION TIME: 20 minutes

MICROWAVE TIME: 22 minutes

SERVES: 4 people

1¾ cups long grain rice
Salt and freshly ground black pepper to taste
3 frozen cod steaks
½lb frozen spinach
2 tblsp butter
3 tblsp milk
3 tblsp canned tuna fish, drained
½ cup Cheddar cheese, cubed
Chopped fresh parsley

Put the rice into a 2-3 quart mixing bowl. Pour on 1¼ pints boiling water. Add ¾ tsp salt. Cover lightly with plastic wrap and pierce once in the centre. Microwave on Full Power for 12 minutes. Set aside. Snip the fish packets open and microwave all 3 together, arranged on a dinner plate in a ring, for 6 minutes on Defrost. Turn each packet over, halfway through cooking. Set aside. Pierce the packet of spinach and place in a vegetable dish. Microwave on Full Power for 6 minutes. Set aside. Slip the cod steaks out of their packets and arrange on a pie plate in a ring. Dot with butter. Season and spoon over the milk. Cover with plastic wrap and pierce. Microwave on Full Power for 4 minutes. Drain the spinach. Chop and fork into the cooked rice. Add the tuna fish to the rice with the cheese. Drain the cooked cod and flake into the rice. Pile onto a warmed dish and serve, sprinkled with plenty of chopped parsley.

JACKET POTATOES WITH FILLINGS

Plain Jacket Potatoes

PREPARATION TIME: 15-20 minutes

MICROWAVE TIME: 15 minutes

SERVES: 4 people

4 x 7oz potatoes, scrubbed clean

Prick the potatoes with a fork and arrange in a ring on a dinner plate. Microwave uncovered, on Full Power, for 15 minutes. Wrap in a clean tea towel and set aside for 10-15 minutes. (The potatoes will continue to cook). Meanwhile prepare one of the fillings (all fillings serve 4 people).

Cottage Cheese with Prawns and Chives

Instead of pricking the potatoes, make a cross in the top of each one before baking.
2 cups cottage cheese
2 tblsp chopped chives
1 cup peeled prawns
2 tblsp soured cream
1½ tsp tomato paste
Sliced cucumber and whole prawns to garnish

Blend all the ingredients together, apart from the cucumber and prawns. Using a cloth, carefully push up each hot potato from the base, to form a water lily. Divide the filling between the potatoes. Garnish with the cucumber and whole prawns before serving.

Pilchards with Corn

3 tblsp natural yogurt or mayonnaise
Salt and freshly ground black pepper to taste
12oz pilchards in tomato sauce
4 tblsp drained canned corn kernels
4 scallions, chopped

Cut the potatoes in half and carefully scoop out the flesh, leaving the skin intact. Put the potato flesh into a 2 quart mixing bowl. Mash well with a fork, adding the yogurt or mayonnaise and salt and pepper to taste. Open each pilchard and remove the backbone. Flake the pilchards into the potato; mix well, adding the corn and chopped scallions. Pile the mixture back into the potato shells. Arrange in a serving dish. Cover with plastic wrap. Microwave on Full Power for 4 minutes.

Baked Beans with Edam Cheese

16oz can baked beans in tomato sauce
2 cups Edam cheese, cubed
Salt and freshly ground black pepper to taste

Garnish
Watercress

Empty the beans into a 2 pint casserole dish. Add the cheese and salt and pepper to taste. Cover with a lid and microwave on Power 7, or Roast, for 2½ minutes. Stir gently. Microwave on Power 7, or Roast, for 2½ minutes. Halve the potatoes after their standing time. Spoon the beans and cheese onto the potatoes. Garnish with watercress and serve.

Stuffed Baked Peppers (top), Jacket Potatoes with Fillings (center) and Garlic Mushrooms (bottom).

Supper Dishes

Shish Kebabs

PREPARATION TIME: 10 minutes
MICROWAVE TIME: 8 minutes
SERVES: 3-4 people

12oz raw ground lamb
1 onion, finely chopped
2½ tsp lemon juice
3 tsp hot curry powder
1½ tblsp soured cream
½ egg, beaten
¼ cup all purpose flour
3 tblsp finely chopped fresh parsley
½ tsp salt
2 tblsp tomato sauce

Mix all the ingredients together. Form the mixture into small balls. Arrange the meatballs on a microwave roasting rack in a ring. Microwave, uncovered, on Power 7, or Roast, for 8 minutes. Serve hot with yogurt sauce.

Yogurt Sauce

PREPARATION TIME: 5 minutes
SERVES: 4 people

⅔ cup natural yogurt
1½ tsp granular mustard
3 tsp tomato paste
1½ tsp concentrated mint sauce
1½ tsp lemon juice
1½ tsp superfine sugar
2½ tblsp soured cream

Mix all the ingredients together until well blended. Refrigerate until required. Serve with Shish Kebabs.

Pasta Shells with Cheese and Bacon

PREPARATION TIME: 15 minutes
MICROWAVE TIME: 24 minutes
SERVES: 4 people

6oz dried pasta shapes
½ tsp salt
1¼ tblsp oil
8oz packet frozen mixed vegetables
1¼ tsp cornstarch
1¼ cups milk
1¼ tsp made mustard
Salt and freshly ground black pepper to taste
¾ cup grated mild hard cheese
2 bacon chops
1 Recipe Crispy Topping (see recipe)

Place the pasta in a 3-4 quart mixing bowl. Add the salt and the oil. Pour on 2 quarts boiling water. Cover tightly with plastic wrap and pierce once in the centre. Microwave on Full Power for 8 minutes. Set aside, covered. Microwave the pierced packet of vegetables in a suitable dish, for 4 minutes on Full Power, turning the packet over once halfway through the cooking time. Blend the cornstarch with 1½ tblsp milk until smooth. Put the remaining milk into a 2¼ pint jug and microwave on Full Power for 3 minutes. Beat the blended cornstarch into the hot milk together with the mustard and salt and pepper to taste. Microwave on Full Power for 2 minutes. Beat well adding the cheese. Microwave the bacon chops on 2 sheets of absorbent kitchen paper (with the fat facing outwards). Microwave on Roast for 4 minutes. To assemble the dish: drain the pasta and pile onto a serving dish; drain the vegetables and add to the pasta; chop the bacon and mix into the pasta and vegetables. Pour the cheese sauce evenly over the top and top with crispy crumbs. Microwave on Power 5, or Roast, for 3 minutes. Serve immediately.

Fish Fingers

PREPARATION TIME: 5 minutes
MICROWAVE TIME: 14 minutes
SERVES: 3-4 people

2½ tblsp cooking oil
8 frozen cod fish fingers

Preheat a large browning dish, without a lid, for 7 minutes, on Full Power. Put the oil into the heated dish. Microwave on Full Power for 1 minute. Carefully press the fish fingers into the oil. Microwave, uncovered, on Full Power for 3 minutes. Turn each fish finger over and microwave on Full Power for 3-4 minutes. Drain on absorbent kitchen paper and serve immediately (brown side uppermost).

Crispy Topping

PREPARATION TIME: 10 minutes
MICROWAVE TIME: 8 minutes

5 tblsp butter
1 cup fresh brown breadcrumbs
½ cup oatmeal

Put the butter into a 2 quart mixing bowl and microwave on Full Power for 1½ minutes. Stir in the breadcrumbs and oatmeal. Microwave on Full Power for 2½ minutes. Stir with a fork. Microwave on Full Power for 2 minutes. Stir. Microwave on Full Power for 2 minutes. Allow to stand for 5 minutes before using. Alternatively, the topping may be cooled and stored in an air tight container. Serve as a crispy finish for sweet and savory dishes.

Kidney and Sausage Supper Dish

PREPARATION TIME: 20 minutes
MICROWAVE TIME: 18 minutes
SERVES: 4 people

1lb chipolata sausages
2½ tblsp oil
8oz lambs' kidneys, skinned, halved and cored
3 tblsp tomato sauce
1½ tblsp Worcestershire sauce
Salt and freshly ground black pepper to taste
4 large, ripe tomatoes, skinned and chopped
8oz frozen peas
2½ tsp cornstarch

Preheat the deep browning dish, without the lid, for 4-7 minutes according to size. Prick the sausages and cut into 1 inch pieces. Add the oil and the pieces of sausage to the preheated dish, pressing the sausage against the sides of the browning dish. Microwave on Full Power for 2 minutes. Stir in the kidneys, tomato sauce and Worcestershire sauce. Cover with the lid and microwave on Power 7, or on Roast, for 5 minutes. Season with salt and pepper and stir in the tomatoes and peas. Mix the cornstarch to a smooth paste with 5 tblsp water and stir in. Microwave on Full Power for 2 minutes. Stir. Microwave on Full Power for a further 2 minutes. Stir and serve immediately.

Cowboy Supper

PREPARATION TIME: 15 minutes
MICROWAVE TIME: 13 minutes
SERVES: 4 people

16oz can baked beans
7oz can corned beef, chilled
Freshly ground black pepper to taste
½ beef stock cube, crumbled
½ cup Cheddar cheese, cubed
1 French loaf

Empty the baked beans into a 2 quart casserole dish. Cover with a lid. Microwave on Power 6 for 5 minutes. Gently stir in the corned beef and season with pepper. Add the stock cube. Cover and microwave on Power 6 for 5 minutes. Add the cheese just before serving.
To warm the bread, cut the bread into pieces and arrange in a bread basket, between absorbent paper napkins. Microwave on Power 4, or Simmer, for 3 minutes. Serve immediately.

Shish Kebabs with Yogurt Sauce (top), Pasta Shells with Cheese and Bacon (center right) and Kidney and Sausage Supper Dish (bottom).

Poached Eggs on Cheese on Toast

PREPARATION TIME: 10 minutes

MICROWAVE TIME: about 10 minutes

SERVES: 4 people

4 eggs
Salt and freshly ground black pepper to taste
Softened butter
4 slices toast
1¼ cups grated cheese
Chopped chives

Put 1½ tblsp cold water into each of the 4 hollows of a microwave muffin pan or into 4 ramekin dishes. If using ramekins, arrange them in a ring on a dinner plate.

Microwave on Full Power until the water boils. Carefully crack 1 egg into each hollow or dish. Prick each yolk once with a cocktail stick. Season with salt and pepper. Microwave on Simmer for about 4 minutes until the whites are just set. Leave aside. Butter the toast and top with the grated cheese. Microwave on Power 5, or Simmer, for about 4 minutes until melted. Slide the toasted cheese onto a serving dish and place an egg on top of each one. Sprinkle with chopped chives and serve immediately.

Cod and Prawn Supper Dish

PREPARATION TIME: 15 minutes

MICROWAVE TIME: 15½ minutes

SERVES: 4 people

4 x 3oz frozen cod steaks, thawed
4 tblsp butter
Salt and freshly ground black pepper to taste
¼ cup flour
1¼ cups milk
¾ cup grated Cheddar cheese
1 cup peeled prawns
1 Recipe Crispy Topping (see recipe)

Garnish
Tomato wedges
Parsley

Arrange the fish steaks in a ring on a dinner plate. Divide half the butter into 4; put a small knob onto each fish steak. Season with salt and pepper and cover with plastic wrap. Microwave on Full Power for 3½ minutes. Set aside. Microwave the remaining butter in a 2¼ pint jug for 1 minute on Full Power. Stir in the flour and then gradually stir in the milk; season to taste. Microwave on Full Power for 2 minutes. Beat well. Microwave on Full Power for a further 2 minutes. Beat in the cheese. Cut the fish into bite-size pieces and arrange in a suitable dish with the prawns. Pour the sauce evenly over the fish. Sprinkle with the crispy crumbs. Microwave on Power 4 for 7 minutes. Serve immediately, garnished with tomato and parsley.

Chicken with Ham

PREPARATION TIME: 15 minutes

MICROWAVE TIME: 13 minutes

SERVES: 4 people

3 cups cooked chicken, roughly chopped
1 cup cooked ham, chopped
5 tblsp drained canned corn kernels with peppers
2 tblsp butter
4 tblsp flour
Salt and freshly ground black pepper to taste
1¼ cups well flavored chicken stock
¾ cup grated cheese
4 tblsp light cream

Garnish
Sliced tomato and parsley

Arrange the chicken, ham and corn in a suitable dish. Melt the butter in a large jug for about 1 minute on Full Power. Stir in the flour and salt and pepper to taste. Stir in a little of the stock, blending it in well. Add the remaining stock. Microwave on Full Power for 2 minutes. Beat well with a wire whisk. Microwave on Full Power for 2 minutes. Beat well. Beat in the cheese and the cream. Pour the sauce evenly over the meat. Microwave on Power 4, or Simmer, for about 8 minutes. Serve immediately, garnished with the tomato and parsley.

Sweet and Sour Pork

PREPARATION TIME: 25 minutes

MICROWAVE TIME: 29 minutes

SERVES: 4 people

1¼ tblsp oil
½ red pepper, de-seeded and chopped
1 carrot, peeled and cut into strips
1 large onion, sliced
4 inch cucumber, seeded and cut into strips
1 stalk celery, chopped
1lb pork fillet, cubed
14oz can pineapple pieces in natural juice
2½ tblsp soya sauce

Fish Fingers (top right), Poached Eggs on Cheese on Toast (far left) and Chicken with Ham (left).

2½ tsp tomato paste
1¼ tblsp wine vinegar
Salt and freshly ground black pepper
   to taste
2½ tsp cornstarch

Preheat the deep browning dish
without the lid for 4-7 minutes

according to size on Full Power. Put
the oil, pepper, carrot, onion,
cucumber and celery into the dish.
Stir well. Cover and Microwave on
Full Power for 4 minutes. Stir in all
remaining ingredients, apart from
the cornstarch. Cover and
microwave on Full Power for 3

minutes and then on Power 4, or
Simmer, for 20 minutes. Cream the
cornstarch with a little water and
stir into the pork mixture.
Microwave on Full Power for 2
minutes. Stir and then serve
immediately on a bed of rice.

**Cowboy Supper (top) and
Sweet and Sour Pork (bottom).**

Fish Dishes

Plaice with Lemon

PREPARATION TIME: 12-15 minutes

MICROWAVE TIME: 9 minutes

SERVES: 4 people

4 plaice fillets (about 3½oz each), skinned
Salt and freshly ground black pepper to taste
Juice of ½ a lemon
3 tblsp milk
1 cup mushrooms, sliced
2 tblsp butter
½ cup soured cream

Lay the plaice fillets out flat; season with salt and pepper and sprinkle with lemon juice. Roll up and secure with wooden cocktail sticks. Arrange the fillets close together in a dish and spoon over the milk; cover and microwave on Full Power for 5 minutes. Set aside. Put the mushrooms and butter into a small dish. Cover and microwave on Full Power for 2 minutes. Add the soured cream and stir in the juices from the fish. Microwave on Full Power for 2 minutes. Arrange the fish on a warmed serving dish. Pour over the sauce and serve immediately.

Curried Prawns with Chicken

PREPARATION TIME: 15 minutes

MICROWAVE TIME: about 22 minutes

SERVES: 4 people

4 tblsp butter
1 medium onion, finely chopped
5 tsp flour
5 tsp mild curry powder
2½ tsp tomato paste
3¾ cups boiling chicken stock
1¼ tblsp apple chutney
1 banana, thinly sliced
¼ cup raisins
Salt and freshly ground black pepper to taste
8oz peeled prawns
8oz cooked chicken, chopped
2½ tblsp lemon juice

Place the butter in a 3 quart

casserole dish. Microwave on Full Power for 1-2 minutes. Stir in the onion. Microwave on Full Power for 1½ minutes. Stir in the flour and curry powder. Microwave on Full Power for 2 minutes. Stir in the tomato paste and gradually add the stock. Add the apple chutney,

banana, raisins and salt and pepper to taste. Cover and microwave on Full Power for 12 minutes. Stir in the peeled prawns, chicken and lemon juice. Microwave on Full Power for 3-4 minutes.

Curried Prawns with Chicken (top left), Scampi Italienne (top right) and Plaice with Lemon (bottom).

Scampi Italienne

PREPARATION TIME: 10 minutes

MICROWAVE TIME: 10 minutes

SERVES: 4 people

½ red pepper, de-seeded and sliced
½ green pepper, de-seeded and sliced
4 tblsp butter
1 small onion, finely chopped
1 clove garlic, crushed
⅔ cup dry white wine
1½ tblsp lemon juice
Salt and freshly ground black pepper
 to taste
1lb frozen shelled scampi, thawed

Garnish
Lemon butterflies
Savory

Put the red and green peppers, butter, onion and the garlic into a 2 quart casserole dish. Cover with the lid. Microwave on Full Power for 3 minutes. Stir in the white wine, lemon juice, salt and pepper to taste and the scampi. Cover and microwave on Full Power for 6-7 minutes, stirring once halfway through. Serve immediately, garnished with lemon butterflies and savory.

Special Fish Pie

PREPARATION TIME: 15 minutes

MICROWAVE TIME: 15 minutes

SERVES: 4 people

1lb young leeks, washed and cut into
 1½ inch lengths
4 large, firm tomatoes, skinned and
 sliced
3 tsp mixed dried herbs
2 tblsp butter
Salt and freshly ground black pepper
 to taste
¾lb cod, skinned and filleted
3 tblsp frozen corn kernels, thawed
½ cup grated Cheddar cheese
1½ tblsp tomato sauce
1lb potatoes, peeled, cooked and
 mashed

Arrange the leeks and tomatoes in the base of a casserole dish; sprinkle with half the herbs. Dot the butter over the surface and season well with salt and pepper. Cover and microwave on Full Power for 5 minutes. Cut the fish into 1 inch pieces. Arrange evenly over the vegetables and season once again. Cover and microwave on Full Power for 7 minutes. Drain off excess liquid and add the corn. Add the cheese, tomato sauce and remaining herbs to the potato; beat well. Pile or pipe the potato on top of the fish and vegetables. Microwave, uncovered, on Full Power for about 3 minutes. Brown under a pre-heated broiler, if desired, and serve immediately.

Mackerel with Apple Sauce

PREPARATION TIME: 30 minutes

MICROWAVE TIME: 15 minutes

SERVES: 4 people

4 fresh mackerel, heads and fins
 removed, and filleted (approx. 6oz
 per fish)
1 cup fresh brown breadcrumbs
1 eating apple, peeled, cored and
 chopped
½ cup shredded suet
1½ tsp lemon juice
3 tsp finely chopped fresh parsley
1 onion, peeled and finely chopped
Salt and freshly ground black pepper
 to taste
1 egg, beaten
3 tblsp apple juice

Sauce
1½lb cooking and eating apples
 (mixed), peeled, cored and sliced
2½ tsp lemon juice
3 tsp superfine sugar
1 tblsp butter

Put the breadcrumbs, apple, suet, lemon juice, parsley and onion into a mixing bowl. Season to taste with salt and pepper. Mix with the beaten egg to bind. Divide the stuffing among the fish, pressing it well into each cavity. Make an incision with a sharp knife in the thickest side of each fish. Arrange the fish, nose to tail, in a shallow dish. Pour over the apple juice. Cover tightly with plastic wrap and pierce. Microwave on Full Power for 8 minutes. Stand on one side while preparing the sauce. Put the apples into a 2 quart mixing bowl with the lemon juice and sugar. Cover. Microwave on Full Power for 6-7 minutes. Allow to stand for 3 minutes. Beat together with the butter and the juices from the cooked fish. Serve immediately with the fish.

Trout with Almonds

PREPARATION TIME: 10 minutes

MICROWAVE TIME: about
 19 minutes

SERVES: 4 people

4 rainbow trout, cleaned and gutted
 (approx 8oz per fish)
5 tblsp butter
1 clove garlic, crushed
Salt and freshly ground black pepper
 to taste
1 cup heavy cream
½ cup flaked almonds

Garnish
Fresh parsley

Use a very small amount of foil to mask the tail of each fish. Make 2 incisions in the thick side of each fish. Put 4 tblsp of the butter into a suitable shallow dish and microwave on Full Power for 1½ minutes. Stir the garlic and salt and pepper into the butter. Arrange the fish, nose to tail, in the flavored butter. Cover with plastic wrap and pierce. Microwave on Full Power for 8 minutes. Turn each fish over once during cooking. Stand aside, covered. Put the almonds and the remaining butter into a soup bowl. Microwave on Full Power for 2 minutes. Stir. Microwave on Full Power for a further 2 minutes. Pour the cream over the fish, and microwave on Power 4 or, Simmer, for 5 minutes. Serve immediately sprinkled with the toasted nuts and garnished with parsley.

Devilled Herrings

PREPARATION TIME: 15-20
 minutes

MICROWAVE TIME: 6-7 minutes

SERVES: 4 people

2½ tblsp dry mustard
1¼ tblsp brown sugar
1¼ tblsp malt vinegar
4 fresh herrings, about 8oz each
½ cup white wine
1 medium onion, finely chopped
1½ tblsp finely chopped fresh parsley
Salt and freshly ground black pepper
 to taste
2 tblsp butter

Blend together the mustard, sugar and vinegar. Cut the heads and the tails off the fish and remove the back-bones; flatten each fish. Spread the mustard mixture inside the herrings and roll up. Secure with cocktail sticks. Arrange the fish in a suitable dish. Add the wine, parsley and salt and pepper to taste. Dot with butter. Cover tightly with plastic wrap or a lid. Pierce if using plastic wrap. Microwave on Full Power for 6-7 minutes. Stand for 3 minutes before serving.

Smoked Haddock with Scrambled Eggs

PREPARATION TIME: 5-10
 minutes

MICROWAVE TIME: 11 minutes

SERVES: 3-4 people

1lb smoked haddock fillet
Salt and freshly ground black pepper
 to taste
⅔ cup milk
4 tblsp butter
4 eggs
1½ tblsp finely chopped fresh parsley

Arrange the fish in a shallow container. Season with salt and pepper and add 2½ tblsp of the milk. Dot the fish with half the butter. Cover with plastic wrap and pierce. Microwave on Full Power for 7 minutes. Set aside, covered. Make the scrambled egg: beat the eggs with the remaining milk in a 2 quart mixing bowl; season to taste and add the remaining butter. Microwave on Full Power for 2 minutes; beat well, using a wire whisk. Microwave on Full Power for 2 minutes until light and fluffy. Carefully arrange the fish on a serving dish. Spoon the scrambled eggs either side of the fish. Sprinkle with the chopped parsley and serve immediately.

Special Fish Pie (top), Mackerel with Apple Sauce (center) and Trout with Almonds (bottom).

Prawns Creole

PREPARATION TIME: 15 minutes
MICROWAVE TIME: 18 minutes
SERVES: 4 people

1¾ cups long grain rice
2½ cups boiling chicken stock
2 medium size onions, chopped
½ red pepper, de-seeded and chopped
½ green pepper, de-seeded and
    chopped

8oz peeled prawns
15oz can pineapple segments in
    natural juice, drained
¼ cup seedless raisins
Salt and freshly ground black pepper
    to taste

Put the rice into a 2-3 quart mixing bowl. Pour on the boiling stock. Cover tightly with plastic wrap and pierce once in the centre. Microwave on Full Power for 12 minutes. Set aside, covered with a clean tea towel. Put the onion and red and green pepper into a 2 pint mixing bowl. Cover with plastic wrap and pierce. Microwave on Full Power for 3 minutes. Stir. Fork up the rice after 10 minutes standing time, and add the onions, peppers, prawns, pineapple, raisins and salt and pepper. Cover with plastic wrap and pierce. Microwave on Full Power for 3 minutes to reheat. Serve immediately.

Smoked Haddock with
Scrambled Eggs (below left),
Prawns Creole (below) and
Devilled Herrings (below
right).

Meat Dishes

Sausagemeat Stuffing

PREPARATION TIME: 15 minutes

MICROWAVE TIME: 10 minutes

SERVES: 4 people

1lb pork sausagemeat
¾ cup parsley and thyme mixed
1¼ tblsp tomato sauce
1¼ tsp made mustard
1 small onion, finely chopped
Salt and freshly ground black pepper
    to taste
⅔ cup boiling water

Put the sausagemeat into a 2 quart mixing bowl. Add all the remaining ingredients. Leave to stand for 3 minutes. Knead toether until well mixed. Using dampened hands, form the sausagemeat mixture into 20 balls. Arrange on a large roasting rack, or in a ring on a large circular dish, on 2 sheets of absorbent kitchen paper. Microwave on Power 7, or Roast, for 10 minutes.

Savory Ground Meat with Dumplings

PREPARATION TIME: 20 minutes

MICROWAVE TIME: 23 minutes

SERVES: 4 people

2 rashers bacon, de-rinded and
    chopped
1 medium onion, chopped
½ green pepper, de-seeded and
    chopped
1½lb raw ground beef or pork
1 beef stock cube, crumbled
1 tsp mixed dried herbs
⅔ cup water
1½ tsp chive mustard
Salt and freshly ground black pepper
    to taste
16oz can navy beans (or white
    kidney beans)

Dumplings
1 cup all purpose flour
1½ tsp baking powder
½ cup suet
½ tsp dried tarragon

Put the bacon, onion and pepper into a soup bowl. Cover with plastic wrap and pierce. Microwave on Full Power for 2 minutes. Put the ground meat into a 2 quart casserole dish. Microwave on Full Power for 4 minutes. Break down with a fork and stir in the onion mixture, stock cube, herbs, water and mustard. Season well with salt and pepper. Microwave on Power 6, or Roast, for 12 minutes. Stir in the beans. Set aside. To prepare the dumplings: mix together the flour, baking powder, suet and tarragon. Bind with sufficient cold water to make an elastic dough. Divide into 6 dumplings and arrange on top of the ground meat. Cover with a lid and microwave on Power 7 for 4-5 minutes. Stand for 3 minutes before serving.

Mixed Meat Loaf

PREPARATION TIME: 30 minutes

MICROWAVE TIME: 27 minutes

SERVES: 6-8 people

1 clove garlic
6oz lean bacon, de-rinded
1lb raw ground beef
8oz raw ground pork
6oz lambs' liver, finely chopped
6oz Canadian bacon, de-rinded and
    finely chopped
½ cup shredded suet
½ cup fresh brown breadcrumbs
½ tsp dried oregano
½ tsp mixed dried herbs
Salt and freshly ground black pepper
    to taste
4 tblsp sherry
1 egg, beaten

Glaze
2½ tblsp apricot jam or marmalade,
    sieved
1 tsp French mustard
½ tsp meat and vegetable extract

Rub a 2 quart plastic meat loaf pan with the clove of garlic. Lay the bacon in the meat loaf pan to line the base and the sides. In a large mixing bowl, mix the ground beef with the pork, liver, Canadian bacon, suet, breadcrumbs and herbs. Season to taste. Beat together the sherry and the egg; add to the mixture and bind together. Transfer to the prepared loaf pan. Smooth the top. Cover and microwave on Power 6, or Roast, for 27 minutes. Turn the dish ½ a turn twice during this time. Allow to stand for 10 minutes. Pour off the excess fat and carefully unmold the loaf. Mix all ingredients together for the glaze and brush over the top and sides of the meat loaf. Delicious hot or cold.

Cheesey Beef Cobbler

PREPARATION TIME: 30 minutes

MICROWAVE TIME: 20 minutes

SERVES: 4 people

1lb raw ground beef
1 onion, chopped
8oz can tomatoes, chopped
1 beef stock cube, crumbled
1¼ tblsp bottled brown sauce
Celery salt and freshly ground black
    pepper to taste
2½ tblsp frozen peas

Scone Topping
2 cups flour, sieved with 1½ tsp
    baking powder
4 tblsp margarine or butter, chilled
½ cup grated Cheddar cheese
1 tsp mixed dried herbs
1 egg, mixed with ½ cup milk
1½ tsp meat and vegetable extract

Put the ground meat and onion into a 7 inch souffle dish. Cover and microwave on Full Power for 4 minutes. Stir well with a fork. Stir in the toatoes, stock cube, brown sauce and celery salt and pepper. Cover and microwave on Power 7, or Roast, for 10 minutes. Stir in the peas and set aside. Put the flour and baking powder into a 2 quart mixing bowl. Blend in the margarine or butter. Mix in the cheese and herbs. Add the beaten egg and milk and mix to a soft dough. Knead lightly. Roll the dough out to a thickness of ½ inch. Using a 2 inch pastry cutter, cut the dough into scones. Arrange the scones on top of the ground meat. Cook, uncovered, on Full Power for 6 minutes. Serve immediately. Note: to improve the color of the scones mix the meat and vegetable extract with a little water and use to brush the scones prior to cooking.

Lamb Curry

PREPARATION TIME: 20 minutes

MICROWAVE TIME: about 45
                 minutes

SERVES: 4 people

2 carrots, peeled and chopped
1 medium onion, chopped
2 tblsp butter
¼ cup all purpose flour
4-5 tsp mild curry powder
1lb lamb fillet, cubed
1¾ cups boiling chicken stock
1¼ tblsp shredded coconut
¼ cup white raisins
1 medium sized eating apple, peeled,
    cored and chopped
1 peach, peeled, stoned and roughly
    chopped
1¼ tomato paste
2½ tblsp lemon juice
Salt and freshly ground black pepper
    to taste

Preheat a large browning dish, without the lid, for 3 minutes on Full Power. Put the carrots, onion and butter into the preheated dish. Microwave on Full Power for 2 minutes, covered. Stir in the flour, curry powder and meat. Microwave on Full Power for 4 minutes. Gradually add the stock, stirring all the time. Stir in the coconut, white raisins, apple, peach, tomato paste, lemon juice and seasoning to taste. Cover and

Lamb Curry (top left), Savory Ground Meat with Dumplings (top right) and Mixed Meat Loaf (bottom).

microwave on Full Power for 7 minutes. Stir. Microwave on Power 4, Simmer or Defrost, for 30-35 minutes. Stir twice during this time. Serve immediately.

Pasta with Pork and Liver

PREPARATION TIME: 15 minutes
MICROWAVE TIME: 25 minutes
SERVES: 4 people

2½ tblsp oil
1 medium onion, sliced
12oz raw ground pork
4oz chicken livers, ground
1 cup mushrooms, chopped
8oz can tomatoes, chopped
4 tblsp sherry
Salt and freshly ground black pepper to taste
1 beef stock cube, crumbled

6oz dried pasta shells
Chopped fresh parsley

Heat the browning dish, without the lid, for 4-6 minutes on Full Power, according to size. Put half the oil, the onion and ground meats into the preheated dish. Stir well. Microwave on Full Power for 4 minutes. Stir in all the remaining ingredients, apart from the pasta and the parsley. Cover with the lid and microwave on Full Power for 3 minutes. Stir. Microwave, covered, on Power 5, or Simmer, for 10 minutes. Allow to stand whilst preparing the pasta. To cook the pasta, place the remaining oil and the pasta into a 3-4 quart bowl. Add 2 quarts water and ½ tsp salt to the pasta. Cover and microwave on Full Power for 8 minutes. Allow to stand for 5 minutes. Drain the pasta and arrange on a serving dish. Spoon the meat sauce evenly over the pasta, and garnish with chopped parsley. Serve immediately.

Pasta with Pork and Liver (far left), Cheesey Beef Cobbler (below) and Sausagemeat Stuffing (below right).

Chicken Breasts in Garlic Cream Sauce

PREPARATION TIME: 10 minutes

MICROWAVE TIME: 17 minutes

SERVES: 4 people

4 tblsp butter
1 clove garlic, crushed
1 medium onion, sliced
2 rashers bacon, de-rinded and chopped
½ cup mushrooms, sliced
½ tsp dried basil
Salt and freshly ground black pepper to taste
4 chicken breasts, skinned and boned (about 5oz each)
1 cup heavy cream

Garnish
Savory
Toasted flaked almonds

Melt the butter in a 2 quart casserole dish for 1-2 minutes on Full Power. Stir in the garlic, onion, bacon, mushrooms, basil and salt and pepper to taste. Cover and microwave on Full Power for 2 minutes. Arrange the chicken breasts on top of the vegetables. Cover and microwave on Power 7, or Roast, for 10 minutes. Season the cream and pour evenly over the top to coat. Garnish with savory and almonds. Serve immediately.

Chicken Casserole

PREPARATION TIME: 15 minutes

MICROWAVE TIME: about 40 minutes

SERVES: 4 people

4 chicken portions, skinned (about 8oz each)
2 tblsp butter
1 onion, finely chopped
2 stalks celery, chopped
2 carrots, chopped
2 tblsp drained canned corn kernels
2 tsp cornstarch
1¼ cups chicken stock
Salt and paprika to taste

Put the butter into a 3 quart casserole dish. Microwave on Full Power for 1 minute. Stir in the onion, celery and carrots. Cover with a lid and microwave on Full Power for 3 minutes. Pour the stock into the casserole, and add salt to taste. Arrange the chicken pieces on top of the vegetables, keeping the thickest part to the outside of the dish. Sprinkle each chicken piece with a little paprika. Microwave, covered, on Full Power for 4 minutes. Stir. Microwave on Power 4, Simmer or Defrost, for a further 30 minutes. Using a draining spoon, transfer the chicken to a warmed serving dish. Cover with a piece of foil and set aside. Cream the cornstarch with a little water and stir into the casserole dish. Microwave on Full Power for 2-3 minutes, until boiling and thickened. Stir in the corn. Serve the chicken pieces with the vegetable sauce spooned over the top.

Sausage Suet Pudding

PREPARATION TIME: 30 minutes

MICROWAVE TIME: 21 minutes

SERVES: 4 people

Filling
8oz pork sausages, cut into 1 inch pieces
8oz chicken livers, roughly chopped
¼ cup seasoned flour
1 tblsp oil
1 medium onion, chopped
½ green pepper, de-seeded and chopped
1¼ cups well flavored boiling stock
Salt and freshly ground black pepper to taste

Suet Pastry
2 cups all purpose flour
½ tsp salt
2 tsp baking powder
1 cup finely grated (or shredded) suet
⅔ cup water

Toss the sausages and chicken livers in the seasoned flour. Put the oil into a 2 quart mixing bowl. Microwave on Full Power for 2 minutes. Stir in the onion and green pepper. Microwave on Full Power for 2 minutes. Stir the chicken livers and sausage into the onion. Cover and microwave on Power 8, or Roast, for 5 minutes. Carefully stir in the boiling stock and salt and pepper to taste. Microwave on Full Power for 2-3 minutes, until thickened. Stir and set aside while preparing the pastry. Sieve the flour, salt and baking powder into a bowl. Stir in the suet and mix to a soft dough with the water. Knead lightly. Roll out ⅔ of the pastry and use to line a greased 2 pint boilable plastic pudding basin. Roll the remaining pastry into a circle. Fill the pastry-lined basin with the filling mixture. Dampen the pastry rim with cold water and top with the circle of pastry. Seal edges. Cut a small slit in the top to allow the steam to escape. Cover loosely with absorbent kitchen paper or plastic wrap. Microwave on Power 7, or Roast, for 9 minutes. Stand for 5 minutes before serving.

Herby Roast Chicken

PREPARATION TIME: about 35 minutes

MICROWAVE TIME: about 36 minutes

SERVES: 6 people

¾ cup fresh brown breadcrumbs
½ cup shredded suet
1 tsp finely chopped fresh parsley
1 tsp finely chopped fresh tarragon
1 eating apple, peeled, cored and chopped
1 tsp lemon juice
Salt and freshly ground black pepper to taste
1 small onion, finely chopped
1 egg, beaten
4lb chicken, giblets removed

Coating
4 tblsp butter
2 tsp chicken seasoning
1 tsp paprika
½ tsp mixed dried herbs

Garnish
Watercress

To make the stuffing, combine the breadcrumbs, suet, parsley, tarragon, apple, lemon juice and seasoning to taste. Put the onion into a small bowl and microwave on Full Power for 1 minute. Add the onion to the other ingredients. Bind together with the beaten egg.

Chicken Casserole (top right), Herby Roast Chicken (top left), Chicken Breasts in Garlic Cream Sauce (bottom right) and Sausage Suet Pudding (bottom left).

Roasting Meats

TYPE OF MEAT	MICROWAVE POWER LEVEL	TIME PER 1lb	INTERNAL TEMPERATURE AFTER MICROWAVING	INTERNAL TEMPERATURE AFTER STANDING
Chops 1. Lamb	Power 7 or Roast (Use pre-heated browning dish)	7-8 minutes	Turn the chops over once during cooking time.	
2. Pork	Power 7 or Roast (Use pre-heated browning dish)	9-10 minutes	Allow to stand for 5-10 minutes before serving.	
Beef (Boned & Rolled)	Power 7 or Roast	5-6 minutes *Rare* 7-8 minutes *Medium* 8-10 minutes *Well done*	130°F 150°F 160°F	140°F 160°F 170°F
Beef on the Bone	Power 7 or Roast	5 minutes *Rare* 6 minutes *Medium* 8 minutes *Well done*	130°F 150°F 160°F	140°F 160°F 170°F
Poultry (Unboned)	Full Power	7 minutes	185°F	190°F
Pork	Power 7 or Roast	10-11 minutes	180°F	185°F
Lamb	Power 7 or Roast	8-9 minutes	170°F	180°F

1. Have joints boned and rolled for best results.
2. Use a <u>microwave</u> meat thermostat to gauge when the meat should be removed from the microwave oven.
3. Any joint which is 3lbs or over will brown in the microwave oven, to increase the colouring, use a browning agent before cooking, or flash the meat under a pre-heated hot broiler after standing time.
4. Turn the joint over once during the cooking time.
5. Use a microwave roasting rack, or an upturned saucer, placed in a suitable dish so as to allow the juices to drain.

Stuff the neck end of the bird with the stuffing. Truss. Weigh the stuffed bird and calculate the cooking time accordingly (7 minutes per 1lb). Use small amounts of foil to mask the wings and the stuffed area, to prevent overcooking. Arrange the chicken in a suitable roasting dish, on two upturned saucers, or on a microwave roasting rack. Melt the butter in the microwave for 1 minute on Full Power. Brush the butter all over the chicken. Combine the chicken seasoning, paprika and herbs together and sprinkle all over the chicken. Cover with a split roasta bag. Microwave on Full Power for the calculated time. Allow the chicken to stand, covered with a tent of foil, before serving. Garnish with watercress.

Devilled Pork Chops

PREPARATION TIME: 10 minutes
MICROWAVE TIME: 16 minutes
SERVES: 4 people

2½ tblsp oil
4 loin pork chops (about 6oz each)
A stick of butter
1¼ tblsp dry mustard
2½ tblsp fresh breadcrumbs
1¼ tblsp soya sauce
2½ tsp Worcestershire sauce
1¼ tblsp tomato chutney
Salt and paprika to taste

Preheat the browning dish (without the lid) for 4-7 minutes, according to size, on Full Power. Put the oil into the heated dish and microwave on Full Power for 1

minute. Put the 4 chops into the dish, pressing them down well. Microwave on Full Power for 2 minutes. Turn the chops over and microwave on Power 7, or Roast, for 10 minutes. Combine all the remaining ingredients in a mixing bowl. Spread over the partly cooked chops. Microwave on Power 7, or Roast, for a further 3 minutes.

Beef or Pork Burgers

PREPARATION TIME: 20 minutes
MICROWAVE TIME: 6-7 minutes
SERVES: 4 people

1lb raw ground beef or pork
1 small onion, finely chopped
½ cup fresh breadcrumbs
1 stock cube, crumbled
½ tsp dried parsley
Salt and freshly ground black pepper to taste
1½ tblsp tomato sauce
1¼ tsp made mustard
2 eggs, beaten
4 buns

Mix the ground beef or pork, onion and breadcrumbs together. Add the stock cube and all the other ingredients, apart from the

buns. Mix well. Divide the mixture into 4 and form into burgers. Arrange on a microwave roasting rack, or other suitable dish, in a ring. Microwave on Full Power for 6-7 minutes, turning each burger over once halfway through cooking time. Split the buns and fill with the burgers.

Glazed Leg of Lamb

PREPARATION TIME: 25 minutes
MICROWAVE TIME: about 50 minutes
SERVES: 6 people

4lb leg of lamb
2-3 cloves peeled garlic, cut into thin strips
Salt and freshly ground black pepper to taste
2½ tblsp tomato sauce
1¼ tsp dry mustard
1¼ tsp brown sugar
1 tsp mixed dried herbs

Devilled Pork Chops (top right), Beef or Pork Burgers (center left) and Glazed Leg of Lamb (bottom).

Make incisions all over the joint with a sharp knife; push a strip of garlic into each one. Season with salt and pepper. Combine the tomato sauce, mustard, brown sugar and herbs, and spread evenly over the joint. Arrange the joint on a roasting rack. Cover with a roasta bag. Microwave for 12 minutes on Full Power. Turn the joint over and microwave on Power 4, or Simmer, for 30-40 minutes or until the meat thermometer registers 160°F. Remove the joint. Cover with a tent of foil and allow to stand for 15 minutes before serving.

Rolled Rib Roast of Beef

PREPARATION TIME: 18 minutes	
MICROWAVE TIME: 30 minutes	
SERVES: 6-8 people	

4lb piece rib roast, boned and rolled
Salt and freshly ground black pepper
   to taste
1½ tblsp tomato sauce
1½ tsp soft brown sugar

Stand the joint on the microwave roasting rack, in a suitable dish, keeping the fat side of the meat underneath. Season with salt and pepper. Microwave for 7 minutes, on Full Power. Turn the joint over and microwave on Roast, or Power 7, for 21 minutes. Remove from the microwave. Cover loosely with a tent of foil and allow to stand for 15 minutes. Spread the tomato sauce and brown sugar all over the fat. Microwave on Full Power for 2 minutes. (Check temperatures with a microwave thermometer. See chart).

Barbecue Lamb Chops

PREPARATION TIME: 10 minutes, plus marinating time	
MICROWAVE TIME: 16 minutes	
SERVES: 6 people	

Marinade
2½ tblsp wine vinegar
5 tblsp pure orange juice
1¼ tblsp tomato sauce
1¼ tsp soft brown sugar
1¼ tsp French mustard
½ tsp dried tarragon
1¼ tsp mild curry powder
Salt and freshly ground black pepper
   to taste
1¼ tsp oil
6 loin chops, each about 5oz

Blend all the ingredients together for the marinade, apart from the oil. Lay the chops in a large shallow dish and pour over the marinade. Cover and chill for at least two hours. Turn the chops over in the marinade, once or twice. Preheat a large browning dish for 7 minutes on Full Power. Put the oil and the drained chops into the dish, pressing the chops against the hot dish. Microwave, uncovered, on Full Power for 5 minutes. Turn the chops over. Microwave on Roast, or Power 7, for 3-4 minutes. Serve immediately.

Shepherd's Pie

PREPARATION TIME: 30 minutes	
MICROWAVE TIME: 38 minutes	
SERVES: 4 people	

1 tblsp cooking oil
2 zucchini, thinly sliced
1 small onion, finely chopped
1lb raw lean ground beef
1 tblsp flour
Salt and freshly ground black pepper
   to taste
1 tblsp tomato paste
4 tblsp water
1 beef stock cube, crumbled
2lb potatoes
½ cup milk
1 egg
1 tblsp butter
2 tblsp mild hard cheese, grated

Preheat a small browning dish on Full Power for 3½ minutes (if using a large browning dish preheat on Full Power for 5 minutes). Add the oil, zucchini and onion, and stir. Cover with a lid and microwave on Full Power for 2 minutes. Add the meat and microwave on Full Power for 3 minutes, stirring once. Add the flour, salt and pepper to taste, tomato paste, water and stock cube. Stir well and cover. Microwave on Power 7, or Roast, for 12 minutes, stirring after the first 4 minutes. Remove from the microwave oven and leave to stand. Meanwhile prepare the potatoes. Peel and dice the potatoes. Put them into a roasta bag with 4 tblsp of the milk. Put the bag into a 2 quart bowl. Secure with a rubber band and pierce once at the base. Microwave on Full Power for 17 minutes (turn the bag over once during this time). Stand, covered, for 5 minutes. Drain the potatoes and mash them together with the egg, remaining milk and the butter. Pile the potato onto the meat mixture and sprinkle with the cheese. Microwave on Full Power for 3-4 minutes, until the cheese

Rolled Rib Roast of Beef (top) and Barbecue Lamb Chops (left).

has melted and the pie is very hot. To speed this recipe up you can use reconstituted powdered potato.

Pork with Leeks and Grapes

PREPARATION TIME: 20 minutes

MICROWAVE TIME: 53 minutes

SERVES: 4-5 people

2½ tblsp oil
1 carrot, peeled and sliced
1 stick celery, chopped
8oz potato, peeled and diced
1lb young leeks, washed and sliced
1½lb boned shoulder of pork, cut into
    1 inch cubes
¼ cup all purpose flour
Salt and freshly ground black pepper
    to taste
1¼ cups well flavored chicken stock
1 cup seedless white grapes

Preheat the browning dish for 4 or 7 minutes, according to size. Add the oil, carrot, celery, potato and leeks to the heated dish. Cover with the lid. Microwave on Full Power for 4 minutes. Using a perforated spoon, transfer the vegetables to a dinner plate. Return the browning dish to the microwave, without the lid, for 1 minute on Full Power. Toss the meat in the flour and seasoning; stir into the dish, turning so that all sides come in contact with the hot skillet. Microwave, uncovered, for 3 minutes on Full Power. Stir in the drained vegetables, stock and extra seasoning to taste. Cover with the lid. Microwave, covered, on Power 5, or Simmer, for 40 minutes. Stir in the grapes and serve after a standing time of 5 minutes.

Turkey Fricassee

PREPARATION TIME: 20 minutes

MICROWAVE TIME: 12 minutes

SERVES: 4 people

2 tblsp butter
¼ cup flour
1¼ cups chicken or turkey stock
Salt and freshly ground black pepper
    to taste
1 cup mushrooms, sliced
½ red pepper, de-seeded and chopped
4 rashers bacon, de-rinded and
    chopped

1 medium onion, chopped
12oz cooked turkey, chopped
1 cup stuffed olives, halved
2 tblsp light cream
1 egg yolk

To make the sauce: melt the butter in a 2¼ pint jug for 1 minute on Full Power. Stir in the flour to make a smooth paste. Gradually stir in the stock, mixing well. Season with salt and pepper. Microwave on Full Power for 2 minutes. Beat well with a wire whisk. Microwave on Full Power for 2 minutes. Beat in the sliced mushrooms. Put the red pepper, bacon and onion into a 2½ pint mixing bowl. Cover and microwave on Full Power for 2 minutes. Stir. Arrange the cooked turkey in a serving dish. Add the pepper mixture and most of the halved olives (reserve a few for decoration). Beat the cream and egg yolk into the sauce. Pour the sauce evenly over the vegetables and turkey. Cover with plastic wrap and pierce. Microwave on Power 5 for 5 minutes. Allow to stand for 5 minutes before serving. Garnish with the remaining olives.

Stewed Steak with Garlic

PREPARATION TIME: 25 minutes

MICROWAVE TIME: about 1 hour 40 minutes

SERVES: 4 people

1½lb chuck steak, cubed
1 tblsp seasoned flour
2 leeks, washed and sliced
1 medium onion, sliced
1 carrot, peeled and chopped
2 cloves garlic, crushed
2 tblsp cooking oil
2 rashers bacon, de-rinded and
    chopped
15oz can tomatoes, chopped
1 tblsp tomato paste
Salt and freshly ground black pepper
    to taste
1¼ cups well flavored beef stock
½ tsp dried parsley

Toss the meat in the seasoned flour. Put the leeks, onions, carrot and the garlic into a 2½ pint dish. Cover and microwave on Full Power for 3 minutes. Stir and set aside. Preheat the large browning dish, without the lid, for 7 minutes on Full Power. Pour the oil into the

This page: **Pork with Leeks and Grapes.**

Facing page: **Stewed Steak with Garlic (top), Shepherd's Pie (center right) and Turkey Fricassee (bottom).**

dish and quickly stir in the bacon and the meat. Press the meat against the sides of the dish. Cover and microwave on Full Power for 4 minutes. Stir, and add all the remaining ingredients. Cover. Microwave on Full Power for 4 minutes, and then on Power 4, or Simmer, for 70 minutes. Stir once after the first 30 minutes. Stir, and allow to stand for 10 minutes before serving.

Sauces and Preserves

Basic Savory White Sauce

PREPARATION TIME: 5 minutes
MICROWAVE TIME: 5 minutes
MAKES: ⅔ pint

2 tblsp butter
¼ cup flour
1¼ cups milk or chicken stock
Salt and freshly ground black pepper
   to taste

Melt the butter in a 2¼ pint jug. Microwave on Full Power for 1 minute until very hot. Stir in the flour to form a roux. Gradually stir in all the milk or stock. Season to taste with salt and pepper. Microwave on Full Power for 2 minutes. Beat well with a wire whisk. Microwave on Full Power for 2 minutes. Beat with a wire whisk and serve.

Variations on Basic White Sauce
Cheese Sauce
Beat ½ cup finely grated cheese and 1 tsp made mustard into the

Mushroom Sauce (above right), Basic Savory White Sauce (far right) and Cheese Sauce (right).

finished sauce. The heat of the sauce will melt the cheese.

Mushroom Sauce
Beat ½ cup finely chopped mushrooms into the prepared sauce. The heat of the sauce will cook the mushrooms.

Egg Sauce
Chop 1 hard-boiled egg (cooked conventionally). Beat into the prepared sauce.

Parsley Sauce
Beat 1 tblsp chopped fresh parsley into the finished sauce.

Onion Sauce
Finely chop 1 medium sized peeled onion and put it into a bowl. Cover with plastic wrap and pierce. Microwave on Full Power for 1-1½ minutes to soften. Beat the softened onion into the prepared sauce (the onion should be softened before the sauce is made).

Cranberry Sauce

PREPARATION TIME: 10 minutes
MICROWAVE TIME: 4 minutes
MAKES: about ½ pint

1 orange
8oz frozen cranberries, defrosted
½ cup granulated sugar

Finely grate the rind from the orange into a 2½ pint mixing bowl. Squeeze the juice from the orange and make up to ⅔ cup with cold water. Put the cranberries, sugar, orange juice and water into the mixing bowl. Microwave on Full Power for 4 minutes. Stir once, halfway through cooking time. Stir and serve.

Custard Sauce

PREPARATION TIME: 5 minutes	
MICROWAVE TIME: 4 minutes	
MAKES: 2½ cups	

2 cups milk
½ cup granulated sugar
4 egg yolks
1½ tsp vanilla

Put milk into a 2¼ pint jug and microwave on Full Power for 2 minutes. Beat the egg yolks with the sugar in a 2½ pint mixing bowl until the mixture is a pale lemon colour. Very slowly pour the hot milk onto the egg mixture, stirring constantly, until blended. Pour the mixture back into the jug and microwave on Full Power for 2 minutes. Beat well with a wire whisk. Allow to cool slightly and then stir in the vanilla. Serve hot or cold.

Chocolate Sauce

PREPARATION TIME: 5 minutes	
MICROWAVE TIME: 5 minutes	
MAKES: about ⅔ pint	

2 tblsp butter
1 tblsp cocoa powder
1¼ cups milk
1 tblsp corn syrup

Melt the butter in a 2¼ pint jug for 1 minute on Full Power. Stir in the cocoa, mixing well. Gradually add the milk, stirring. Microwave on Full Power for 2 minutes. Beat well with a wire whisk. Microwave on Full Power for 2 minutes. Beat in the corn syrup. Serve immediately.

Beefy Tomato Sauce

PREPARATION TIME: 10 minutes	
COOKING TIME: 20 minutes	
MAKES: 1¼ pints	

¼ cup butter
2 medium sized onions, finely chopped
½ cup flour
3 cups hot beef stock
2 tblsp tomato paste
1 tblsp vinegar
1 tsp French mustard
1 tsp soft brown sugar
1 tsp Worcestershire sauce

1 tblsp tomato sauce
Salt and freshly ground black pepper to taste

Melt the butter in a really large jug or mixing bowl for 1-2 minutes on Full Power. Stir in the onion and microwave, uncovered, for 3 minutes on Full Power. Stir in the flour, mixing well. Gradually add the stock, stirring continuously. Mix the paste with the vinegar and add to the sauce together with the French mustard, sugar, Worcestershire sauce, tomato sauce and salt and pepper to taste. Microwave on Full Power for 10 minutes. Beat well twice during this time. Turn on to Power 4, or Simmer, and microwave for a further 5 minutes. Beat well. Serve with meat balls, meat loaf, etc.

St. Clement's Sauce

PREPARATION TIME: 10 minutes	
MICROWAVE TIME: 3½ minutes	
MAKES: about ½ pint	

3 tblsp fine cut marmalade
Juice of 1 lemon
Juice of 1 orange
1 tsp arrowroot

Put the marmalade and lemon and orange juices into a 2¼ pint jug. Microwave on Full Power for 1½ minutes. Stir well. Microwave on Full Power for 1 minute. Blend the arrowroot to a smooth paste with a little cold water. Stir into the jug. Microwave on Full Power for 30 seconds. Stir. Microwave on Full Power for a further 30 seconds. Stir and serve.

Plum Jam

PREPARATION TIME: 20 minutes	
MICOWAVE TIME: 1 hour	
MAKES: 2½lb	

Juice of 1 orange
2lb plums, halved and stoned
2lb granulated sugar

Put the juice and the plums into a large microwave container. Cover and microwave on Full Power for 10 minutes. Stir in the sugar to dissolve. Cover and microwave on Power 6 for about 40 minutes, or until setting point is reached. Test for setting. Pot and label in the usual way.

Strawberry Jam

PREPARATION TIME: 20 minutes, plus chilling overnight	
COOKING TIME: 31 minutes	
MAKES: about 2½lb	

2lb freshly picked strawberries, hulled
2lb granulated sugar

Place the hulled strawberries in a 6¼ pint microwave dish. Add the sugar and stir. Cover and leave overnight in the refrigerator. Stir well. Cover and microwave on Full Power for 7 minutes, until boiling point is reached. Microwave on Power 5, or Simmer, for 24 minutes, until setting point is reached. Test for setting. Pot and label in the usual way.

Green Tomato Chutney

PREPARATION TIME: 40 minutes	
MICROWAVE TIME: 1¾-2 hours	
MAKES: about 6lbs	

2 medium onions, finely chopped
1½ cups malt vinegar
1 cup wine vinegar
1 small stalk celery, chopped
½ tsp mustard seed
4lb green tomatoes, washed and chopped
2 large tart cooking apples, peeled, cored and chopped
1½ cups seedless raisins
1 clove garlic, crushed
4 peppercorns, 2 cloves and 2 chilies (tied in muslin)
2 cups soft brown sugar
Salt and freshly ground black pepper to taste

Put the onions into a 6 cup pudding basin. Microwave on Full Power for 2 minutes. Put half the vinegar, the celery, mustard seed, tomatoes, apples, raisins, garlic and onions into a very large bowl.

Parsley Sauce (top), Cranberry Sauce (center left), Onion Sauce (center right) and Egg Sauce (bottom).

Crush the muslin bag with a rolling pin and add to the bowl. Stir. Cover and microwave on Full Power for 10 minutes. Stir in the sugar to dissolve. Add the remaining vinegar and season with salt and pepper to taste. Microwave on Full Power for 20-30 minutes. Remove the lid and stir well. Microwave on Full Power, uncovered, for about 75 minutes until the mixture reduces and thickens. Stir twice during this time. Ladle into clean jam jars. Seal and label when cool. The chutney shld be kept in a cool dark place for 2 months to mature, before using.

This page: Strawberry Jam (top), Plum Jam (center right) and Green Tomato Chutney (bottom).

Facing page: Chocolate Sauce (top), St Clement's Sauce (center left), Beefy Tomato Sauce (center right) and Custard Sauce (bottom).

Sweets

Pear Upside Down Pudding

PREPARATION TIME: 25 minutes

MICROWAVE TIME: 7 minutes

SERVES: 6 people

Oil and superfine sugar
3 tblsp corn syrup
15oz can pear halves, drained
5 glace cherries, halved and rinsed
Recipe quantity Victoria Sandwich
  mixture (see recipe)

Grease a 7 inch souffle dish with oil and sprinkle the base and sides lightly with superfine sugar. Spread the corn syrup over the bottom. Make an attractive pattern over the base with the pears and the glace cherries. Spoon the Victoria Sandwich mixture into the prepared dish. Smooth the top. Microwave on Full Power for 7 minutes. Allow to stand for 7 minutes in the dish before carefully turning out. Serve warm with custard or cream.

Apple and Blackcurrant Flan

PREPARATION TIME: 30 minutes

MICROWAVE TIME: 37 minutes

SERVES: 6 people

Base
1¼ cups white flour
1¼ cups whole-wheat flour
Pinch of salt
¼ cup butter
¼ cup lard
1 egg and 2 tblsp cold water, beaten
  together

Filling
1lb tart cooking apples, peeled, cored
  and sliced
8oz blackcurrants
¼ cup superfine sugar
¾ cup ground almonds
2 tblsp butter
2 egg yolks

Meringue
3 egg whites
¾ cup superfine sugar
Glace cherries and angelica for
  decoration

To make the pastry, sieve the flours and salt into a mixing bowl. Blend the butter and lard until the mixture resembles fine breadcrumbs. Mix to a dough with the egg and cold water. Knead the dough lightly. Roll out and use to line a 10 inch fluted flan dish. Press up pastry to come ¼ inch above the rim of the dish. Prick the sides and base with a fork. Refrigerate for 15 minutes. Using a single strip of foil, about 1 inch wide, line the inside edge of the flan case. Place 2 sheets of absorbent kitchen paper in the base. Weigh down with a few baking beans. Microwave on Full Power for 6 minutes. Remove the foil, beans and absorbent paper. Microwave on Full Power for 2-3

This page: Mille Feuille (top), Apple Mousse (center right) and Pear Upside Down Pudding (bottom).

Facing page: Chocolate Rice Krispie (top), Rhubarb Sunburst (center right) and Creme Caramel (bottom).

minutes. Set aside. Put the fruits into a 2 quart mixing bowl. Cover and microwave on Full Power for about 7-8 minutes, stirring once halfway through. Stir in sugar to dissolve and beat to a puree. Cool. Beat in the ground almonds, butter and egg yolk. Put the egg whites into a large, clean bowl and whisk until stiff and dry. Beat in the sugar, a little at a time, until a thick glossy meringue results. Spread the fruit mixture into the flan case. Pipe or spread the meringue mixture on top to cover completely. Put the flan into a pre-heated moderate oven, 350°F, for 15-20 minutes, until pale golden. Serve sprinkled with tiny pieces of cherry and angelica.

Mille Feuille

PREPARATION TIME: 15-20 minutes, plus cooling time

MICROWAVE TIME: 6 minutes

SERVES: 6 people

8oz puff pastry (you can use a small packet of frozen puff pastry)
8oz fresh strawberries
1¼ cups heavy cream, whipped
2 tblsp superfine sugar
½ cup confectioner's sugar, sieved
Pink food coloring
¼ cup toasted flaked almonds

Roll the pastry out into a circle 8 inches in diameter. Place on a large dinner plate and chill for 10 minutes. Microwave, uncovered, for 5-6 minutes, on Full Power. Turn the plate once halfway through the cooking time. Brown the top under a pre-heated hot broiler for a few seconds, if required. Allow to cool completely. Hull strawberries and roughly chop them. Fold the strawberries into the cream with the superfine sugar. Split the pastry horizontally into 3 layers and place the first layer on a serving dish. Spread thickly with strawberries and cream. Top with the second pastry layer and spread with more strawberries and cream. Add the final layer of pastry, browned side uppermost. Put the confectioner's sugar into a basin. Add a few drops of pink food coloring and just enough boiling water to produce a smooth glace frosting. Spread the frosting over the Mille Feuille using a teaspoon – see picture. Sprinkle with the cold, toasted almonds and serve immediately.

Creme Caramel

PREPARATION TIME: 15 minutes, plus chilling time

MICROWAVE TIME: 28 minutes

SERVES: 4 people

Caramel
¾ cup granulated sugar
½ cup cold water

Custard
1¾ cups milk
4 eggs, lightly beaten
¼ cup superfine sugar

To make the caramel, place the granulated sugar and water into a large jug. Microwave on Full Power for 9-11 minutes, or until a golden caramel results. Swirl the caramel evenly around the inside of a suitable, lightly-greased 2 pint dish. Leave to set. Put the milk into a large, clean jug and microwave on Full Power for 2 minutes. Add the beaten eggs and superfine sugar. Strain onto the set caramel. Cover with plastic wrap and pierce. Stand the dish in a larger container, which will act as a water bath. Pour in sufficient boiling water to come halfway up the sides of the dish containing the creme caramel. Microwave on Power 5, or Simmer, for about 15 minutes or until the custard has set. Remove from the water bath. Carefully peel away the plastic wrap and allow to cool. Chill until ready to serve. Turn out and serve very cold with whipped cream.

Apple Mousse

PREPARATION TIME: 20 minutes

MICROWAVE TIME: 7 minutes

SERVES: 6 people

1½lb tart cooking apples, peeled, cored and sliced
Juice of 1 lemon
3 cubes of lime jelly (from a packet jelly)
3 tblsp superfine sugar
1 cup heavy cream
2 egg whites
1 red-skinned eating apple

Put the prepared cooking apples into a 2 quart casserole dish with half the lemon juice and the lime jelly. Cover with a lid and microwave on Full Power for about 7 minutes until the apples are pulpy (stir once during this time). Beat with a fork, beating in the sugar until melted. Set aside and allow to cool. Blend the cooled

apple in a food processor or liquidizer until smooth. Add the half-whipped cream and process together for a few seconds. Whisk the egg whites in a clean bowl until they stand in soft peaks. Transfer the apple mixture to a large, clean bowl and fold in the beaten egg whites gently. Turn into a serving dish. Decorate with slices of eating apple, which have been brushed with the remaining lemon juice to prevent discoloration.

Rhubarb Sunburst

PREPARATION TIME: 10 minutes, plus chilling time

MICROWAVE TIME: 6 minutes

SERVES: 4 people

1lb fresh young rhubarb, cut into 1 inch pieces
Finely grated rind and juice of 1 orange
1 tblsp apricot jam
6 canned apricot halves, chopped

Place the rhubarb, orange rind and juice, and the jam into a 2 pint mixing bowl. Cover and microwave on Full Power for 6 minutes. Stir. Set aside to cool, and then chill. Stir in the chopped apricots. Serve with natural yogurt, ice cream or whipped heavy cream.

Chocolate Pudding with Cherries

PREPARATION TIME: 10 minutes

MICROWAVE TIME: 8½ minutes

SERVES: 4-6 people

6 tblsp softened butter
6 tblsp soft brown sugar
¾ cup flour
1 tsp baking powder
¼ cup cocoa powder
2 eggs
2 tblsp milk
15oz can cherry pie filling

Put all ingredients, apart from the cherry pie filling, into a mixing bowl. Beat with a wooden spoon for 1 minute. Spoon into a lightly greased 2 pint plastic pudding basin. Microwave on Full Power for 3½-4 minutes, until well risen and springy to the touch. Set aside. Empty the cherry pie filling into a bowl and microwave on Full Power for 3 minutes, stirring after 1½ minutes. Turn the sponge pudding into a dinner plate. Spoon the hot cherry sauce over the top and serve immediately.

Chocolate Rice Krispie

PREPARATION TIME: 15 minutes, plus chilling time

COOKING TIME: 5 minutes

MAKES: 16-20 wedges

A stick of butter
¼ cup superfine sugar
¼ cup cocoa powder
½ cup corn syrup
1 cup Rice Krispies

Lightly grease 2 x 8 inch sandwich tins with a little of the butter (these are not to be used in the microwave). Put the remaining butter, cut into pieces, into a 2 quart mixing bowl with the superfine sugar, cocoa powder and corn syrup. Microwave on Power 5 or Simmer for 4 minutes. Stir halfway through, and again at the end. Microwave on Full Power for a further 1 minute. Stir in the Rice Krispies, making sure that they are all coated with the chocolate mixture. Divide between the prepared tins and smooth level with a knife. Cool and then chill until set. Cut into finger wedges to serve. As an alternative, ½ cup washed, seedless raisins may be stirred in with the Rice Krispies.

Apple Ginger Crisp

PREPARATION TIME: 15 minutes

MICROWAVE TIME: 9 minutes

SERVES: 4-6 people

1lb tart cooking apples peeled, cored and sliced
¼ cup soft light brown sugar
1 tblsp orange juice
5 tblsp butter
2 cups plain ginger biscuits, crushed
½ cup flaked almonds

Place the apples, sugar and orange juice into a 3¼ pint casserole dish. Cover and microwave on Full Power for 4-5 minutes. Stir and set aside. Put the butter into a 2 quart mixing bowl. Microwave on Power 7, or Roast, for about 2 minutes, until melted. Stir the biscuits and almonds into the melted butter. Mix well. Microwave on Full Power for 2 minutes. Stir well with a fork after 1 minute. Carefully spoon the biscuit crumble over the apples. Serve immediately with whipped cream or ice cream. This pudding can also be served cold.

Chocolate Pudding with Cherries (left), Apple Ginger Crisp (below left) and Apple and Blackcurrant Flan (bottom).

Tea Time Treats

Celebration Gateau

PREPARATION TIME: 40 minutes
MICROWAVE TIME: 14 minutes
MAKES: 1 gateau

Cake
Superfine sugar and oil for preparing
the dish
3 eggs
1¼ cups cake flour
¼ cup cocoa powder
1 tsp baking powder
¾ cup softened butter
¾ superfine sugar

Frosting
2 cups confectioner's sugar, sieved
6 tblsp butter
2 tsp boiling water
1 tsp liquid coffee essence
Few drops of vanilla essence

Decoration
1 packet sponge finger biscuits
6oz plain chocolate
1½ yards brown nylon ribbon, 1 inch
wide

Lightly grease a deep, 7 inch diameter souffle dish with oil. Line the base with a circle of wax paper and use a little superfine sugar to dust the sides. Knock out any surplus. Put all the ingredients for the cake into a mixing bowl. Beat for 1 minute. Spoon into the prepared souffle dish and smooth the top. Microwave on Power 7, or Roast, for about 7 minutes, and then on Full Power for 2-3 minutes until the sponge has risen to the top of the souffle dish and is set. Allow to stand in the container for 10 minutes before turning out onto a clean tea towel which has been sprinkled with a little superfine sugar. Cool completely.
To make the frosting: gradually beat the sieved confectioner's sugar into the butter, adding the boiling water. Take 1 tblsp buttercream out of the bowl and beat the coffee essence into it. Beat the vanilla essence into the remaining buttercream. Cut the cake in half horizontally and sandwich together with some of the vanilla buttercream. Spread the vanilla buttercream around the sides and across the top of the cake. Pipe half the cake with vanilla buttercream

and the other half with the coffee buttercream. Arrange the prepared sponge fingers, like soldiers, around the edge of the cake – see picture. Tie brown ribbon around to finish the gateau.
To prepare the sponge fingers: measure 1 sponge finger against the cooked cake. Trim all the sponge fingers to the same size. Break the chocolate into a large mixing bowl and microwave on Power 4 for 3-4 minutes. Stir. Dip the rounded end of the sponge fingers into the melted chocolate to coat the top half of each one. Arrange on a tray and leave in a cool place for 10-15 minutes to set.

Chocolate Frosting

PREPARATION TIME: 5 minutes
MICROWAVE TIME: 2½ minutes

2 tblsp softened butter
1½ tblsp cocoa powder, sieved
1¼ cups confectioner's sugar, sieved
2 tblsp milk

Put the butter and cocoa into a 2½ pint bowl. Microwave on Power 5, or Simmer, for 2½ minutes, until the butter has melted and is very hot. Stir once, halfway through. Beat in the confectioner's sugar and the milk. Beat with a wooden spoon until thick and glossy. Use to coat the top and sides of the cake.

Collettes

PREPARATION TIME: 30 minutes
MICROWAVE TIME: 7½ minutes
MAKES: 12

6oz plain chocolate
2oz milk chocolate
4 tblsp heavy cream
1 tblsp butter
2 tsp brandy or coffee essence
36 paper sweet cases, separated into
twelve groups of three cases

Break the plain chocolate into pieces and put into a 2 pint bowl. Microwave on Power 3, or Defrost,

for 4-5 minutes. Stir. Using a small paint brush or teaspoon, coat the base and sides of each group of paper cases with the melted chocolate. Leave to set. Put the milk chocolate and the butter into a clean bowl. Microwave on Power 3, or Defrost, for 2-2½ minutes. Beat well for a few minutes. Beat in the brandy or coffee essence. Half whip the cream and fold into the milk chocolate mixture using a metal spoon. Chill until firm enough to pipe. Peel the paper cases away from the set chocolate and discard. Pipe rosettes of chocolate filling into the chocolate case. Serve immediately in new paper sweet cases.

Fruit and Almond Cake

PREPARATION TIME: 20 minutes
MICROWAVE TIME: 13-16 minutes
MAKES: 1 cake

Use the large spring clip ring mold, which should be lightly greased and coated with superfine sugar.
¾ cup softened butter
¾ cup soft brown sugar
½ tsp soy sauce
3 eggs, beaten
1½ cups white flour
1½ tsp baking powder
2-3 drops almond essence
¼ cup ground almonds
½ cup seedless raisins
½ cup glace cherries, washed and
roughly chopped

Blend butter and sugar until light and fluffy. Beat in the soy sauce and beaten eggs, a little at a time (add 1 tblsp flour with each addition of egg to prevent curdling). Beat in the almond essence, ground almonds and milk. Fold in the remaining flour, and then the raisins and cherries. Place in the prepared ring mold and smooth the top. Microwave on Power 6, or Roast, for 12-14 minutes, and then on Full Power for 1-2 minutes until just set. Stand for 15 minutes, before turning out. When quite cold, the top may be sprinkled with a little sieved confectioner's sugar.

Cheese and Paprika Scones

PREPARATION TIME: 20 minutes
MICROWAVE TIME: 5-6 minutes
MAKES: about 10

2 cups white flour
2 tsp baking powder
Pinch salt
Pinch paprika
¼ cup firm butter
½ cup mild hard cheese, grated
1 tsp made mustard
1 egg
3 tblsp milk
1 tsp meat extract

Sieve the flour, salt and paprika into a 2 quart mixing bowl. Blend the butter and fork-in the cheese. Beat the mustard and egg together and mix with the milk. Mix into the dry ingredients, using a round bladed knife, to form a soft dough. Knead on a lightly floured board. Roll out to a thickness of ½ inch. Cut into 2½ inch rounds. Arrange the shaped scones in a ring on a non-metallic tray, leaving a gap in the centre. Mix 1 tsp meat extract with a little boiling water and brush over the surface of the scones (do not cover). Microwave immediately on Power 7, or Roast, for 5-6 minutes. Transfer to a cooling rack and allow to stand for 2-3 minutes. Serve hot with butter, or cold if preferred. As an alternative to the meat extract glaze, the cooked scones may be flashed under a pre-heated hot broiler to brown and crisp them.

Celebration Gateau (top),
Collettes (center left) and Fruit
and Almond Cake (bottom).

Microwave Meringues (right),
Victoria Sandwich (below) and
Porridge (bottom right).

Porridge

PREPARATION TIME: 5 minutes

MICROWAVE TIME: 9 minutes

SERVES: 3 people

2 cups milk and water, mixed
½ tsp salt
1 cup oatmeal
6 tblsp soft brown sugar
6 tblsp butter

Put the milk, water and salt into a 2 quart mixing bowl. Stir in the oatmeal. Microwave on Full Power for 3 minutes. Stir. Microwave on Full Power for 3 minutes. Stir. Microwave on Full Power for 3 minutes. Turn into individual serving dishes. Sprinkle with the brown sugar and top with the butter. Serve immediately.

Microwave Meringues

PREPARATION TIME: 20 minutes

MICROWAVE TIME: about 8 minutes

MAKES: 10 sandwiched meringues

1 egg white
12 tblsp confectioner's sugar, sieved
Pink food coloring
1½ cups chocolate buttercream
Chocolate vermicelli

Put the egg white into a 2 quart mixing bowl and beat until frothy. Gradually work in the confectioner's sugar and mix to give a really stiff frosting. Divide the frosting into two portions. Knead a few drops pink food coloring into one portion of frosting. Roll both the frostings separately into small balls, each about the size of a marble. Arrange 4 balls of frosting in a ring on a large dinner plate. Microwave on Full Power for 1½ minutes. Allow to stand for 2 minutes before removing to a cooling tray. Repeat until all the mixture has been cooked. Fill the cooled meringue halves with the chocolate buttercream. Sprinkle with a little vermicelli and serve in paper cake cases.

Victoria Sandwich

PREPARATION TIME: 15 minutes

MICROWAVE TIME: 7 minutes

MAKES: 1 cake

Oil
Superfine sugar for dusting
3 eggs
1½ cups cake flour
1½ tsp baking powder
¾ softened butter
¾ cup superfine sugar
2 drops soy sauce
2 tblsp milk
3 tblsp strawberry jam

Lightly grease a 7 inch souffle dish with oil; dust the sides with a little superfine sugar. Place a circle of wax paper in the base. Put the eggs, flour, butter, sugar, soy sauce and milk into a mixing bowl. Beat for 1 minute. Spoon into the prepared dish and smooth the top. Microwave on Full Power for about 7 minutes. Test by putting a wooden cocktail stick into the centre of the sponge after a 3 minute standing time. The cocktail stick should come out clean. Stand for 10 minutes. Turn out into a wire cooling rack. When quite cold, split in half horizontally. Sandwich together with the jam. Serve with a little superfine sugar sprinkled over the top.

Cream Slices

PREPARATION TIME: 15-20 minutes, plus cooling time

MICROWAVE TIME: 6-8 minutes

MAKES: about 6 slices

8oz puff pastry (small packet frozen puff pastry can be used)
Black cherry jam
3 tblsp confectioner's sugar, sieved
A few drops of pink food coloring

Roll the pastry into an oblong about 4 inches wide and 12-14 inches long. Cut in half, crossways. Dampen the surface of a suitable container. Lift one half of the pastry onto the prepared tray and microwave on Full Power for 3-4 minutes, until well puffed up (when the door is opened, the pastry should hold its shape). Allow to stand for 2-3 minutes and

and just 'set'. Remove from the microwave oven and allow to stand for 5 minutes before turning out. Allow to become quite cold. To make the buttercream, mix the cocoa with 2 tblsp boiling water to form a smooth paste. Beat with the butter and confectioner's sugar until light and creamy. Split the cooled cake in half horizontally. Sandwich together with a little of the buttercream and arrange on a cake board. Use the remaining buttercream to completely coat the 'hedgehog'. Form a 'snout' for his nose. Fork all over. Cut most of the chocolate chips in half and stud the hedgehog with these to represent the prickles. Use 1 chocolate chip for his nose and 2 raisins for his eyes. Spread some green coconut around the base for grass.

Rich Fruit Cake

PREPARATION TIME: 30 minutes	
MICROWAVE TIME: 40 minutes	
MAKES: 1 cake	

½ cup softened butter
½ cup dark soft brown sugar
2 tblsp dark molasses
1 tsp soy sauce
3 eggs
3 tblsp milk
2 cups flour, sieved with 1 tsp mixed spice, a pinch of salt and ½ tsp baking soda
1.2lb mixed dried fruit (white raisins, raisins, currants and peel)
¼ cup chopped blanched almonds
½ cup glace cherries, washed and quartered
3 tblsp sherry or brandy

Lightly grease a deep, 9 inch diameter souffle dish. Line the base with a circle of ungreased wax paper and dust the sides with a little superfine sugar (knocking out any surplus). Beat the butter, sugar,

---

then remove to a cooling tray. Repeat the process with the remaining half of the pastry. Allow to cool. Using a sharp knife, divide each layer into 3 slices. Sandwich each group of three layers together with the jam. Mix the confectioner's sugar with a little boiling water to make a smooth, glossy frosting. Beat in a few drops pink food coloring. Quickly spread the frosting over the top of each layered slice. Cut each one into 3 slices.

Mr. Hedgehog Cake

PREPARATION TIME: 40 minutes	
MICROWAVE TIME: 3½-7 minutes	
MAKES: 1 cake	

6 tblsp softened butter
6 tblsp superfine sugar
1 cup cake flour
2 eggs
1 tblsp milk
1 tblsp cocoa powder
A stick of butter
2 cups confectioner's sugar, sieved
1 packet large milk chocolate chips
2 raisins
Green colored coconut for grass

To make the sponge, put the butter, the superfine sugar, flour, eggs and milk into a mixing bowl. Beat with a wooden spoon for 1 minute. Lightly grease the base and sides of a 2 pint plastic pudding basin. Fill with the sponge mixture and smooth the top. Microwave on Full Power for 3½ minutes, or on Power 6, or Roast, for 6-7 minutes. The sponge should be well risen

This page: Mr. Hedgehog Cake (top), Cream Slice (center left) and Rich Fruit Cake (bottom).

Facing page: Pineapple Gateau (top right), Chocolate Pear Sponge (center left) and Cheese and Paprika Scones (bottom).

molasses and gravy browning in a large mixing bowl until light and fluffy. Gradually beat in the eggs and the milk. Add 1 tblsp flour with each addition of egg, to prevent it curdling. Fold in the remaining flour using a metal spoon. Fold in the fruits, nuts and glace cherries, together with the sherry or brandy. Spoon the mixture into the prepared container. Microwave on Power 4, Simmer or Defrost, for 40 minutes. Remove from the microwave oven and allow to stand in its dish for 20 minutes before turning out. When quite cold, the cake may be covered with almond paste and frosted, or finished with glace fruits, and glazed. Allow the cake to mature for at least 1 month before using.

Date and Walnut Loaf Cake (below) and Crepes Suzette (bottom).

Crepes Suzette

PREPARATION TIME: 25 minutes

MICROWAVE TIME: about 24 minutes

SERVES: 4-6 people

Pancakes
1 cup flour
Pinch salt
1 egg
⅔ cup milk
⅔ cup water
Cooking oil

Sauce
6 tblsp butter
4 tblsp superfine sugar
Grated rind of 1 orange
Grated rind and juice of ½ a lemon
4-5 tblsp brandy or Cointreau

Sieve the flour and salt into a bowl. Make a well in the centre. Add the egg and half of the milk. Beat well. Gradually beat in the remaining milk and the water. Beat in 1 tsp oil. Allow to stand for 10 minutes. Fry the pancakes in the usual way, making 12 pancakes in all. Fold the 12 cooked pancakes in half and then in half again, to form triangles. Arrange in a shallow dish. To make the sauce, put the butter into a 2¼ pint jug and microwave on Defrost for 5 minutes, or until melted and hot. Stir in the sugar to dissolve. Add the fruit rinds, lemon juice, and the brandy or Cointreau. Microwave on Full Power for 2 minutes. Stir. Pour over the pancakes. Cover with plastic wrap and microwave on Power 5, or Simmer, for 5 minutes. Turn each pancake over in the sauce before serving. Serve piping hot.

Pineapple Gateau

PREPARATION TIME: 30 minutes

MICROWAVE TIME: 7 minutes

MAKES: 1 gateau

Oil and superfine sugar
1 recipe quantity Victoria Sandwich mixture (see recipe)
8oz can pineapple slices, drained
1¼ cups heavy cream, whipped
1 cup chopped blanched almonds, toasted
Angelica for decoration

Lightly grease a 7 inch souffle dish or plastic pan with oil. Put a circle of wax paper into the base of the dish; dust the base and sides with superfine sugar (knock out any surplus). Spoon the prepared Victoria Sandwich mixture into the dish, and smooth the surface. Microwave on Full Power for about 7 minutes. Allow to stand for 10 minutes before turning out onto a wire cooling rack. Once the cake is quite cold, remove the wax paper. Split the cake in half horizontally. Chop 1 slice of pineapple and mix with 3 tblsp of the whipped cream; use to sandwich the cake layers together. Spread some of the cream round the sides of the cake and roll it in nuts to coat evenly. Arrange on a serving dish. Spread the top with the remaining cream, piping it if liked. Decorate the top with pineapple and angelica – see picture.

Chocolate Pear Sponge

PREPARATION TIME: 15 minutes

MICROWAVE TIME: 6 minutes

MAKES: 1 sponge cake

14 tblsp cake flour
1 tblsp cocoa powder
1 tsp baking powder
A stick of softened butter
1 tblsp milk
1 tsp mixed spice
4oz ripe pear, peeled, cored and chopped
Oil and superfine sugar for preparing the souffle dish

Put all the ingredients, apart from the pear, into a 2 quart mixing bowl. Mix with a wooden spoon and then beat for 1 minute. Fold in the pear, using a metal spoon. Lightly grease a 7 inch souffle dish; line the base with a circle of wax paper and coat the sides with a little superfine sugar. Turn the mixture into the prepared souffle dish and smooth the top. Microwave on Power 6, or Roast, for 4 minutes, and then on Full Power for 2 minutes. Allow to stand for 10 minutes before turning out onto a cooling rack. The cooling rack should be covered with a clean tea towel, sprinkled with a little superfine sugar. When quite cold, frost the cake with chocolate frosting.

Date and Walnut Loaf Cake

PREPARATION TIME: 15 minutes

COOKING TIME: 6 minutes

MAKES: 1 loaf

2 eggs
4 tblsp milk
1 tblsp corn syrup
1 tsp soy sauce
½ cup softened butter
1½ cups white flour
1½ tsp baking powder
¾ cup soft brown sugar
¾ cup chopped stoned dates
1 small banana, sliced
½ cup walnuts, chopped

Put the eggs, milk, corn syrup, gravy browning, butter, flour and brown sugar into a large mixing bowl. Beat with a wooden spoon. Using a metal spoon, fold in the dates, banana and walnuts. Turn into a lightly greased 2 quart microwave bread baker. Microwave on Full Power for about 6 minutes, turning the dish a half turn, halfway through cooking time. Allow to stand in the bread baker for 10 minutes before turning out. Serve sprinkled with superfine sugar.

Index